TB JOSHUA

SERVANT OF GOD

by

Gary & Fiona Tonge

En Gedi Publishing
United Kingdom

Nothing in this book is intended to discourage anyone from seeking medical
diagnosis or treatment.

Reprint of first edition (preface added) - September 2021

ISBN 978-1-9168991-0-0

En Gedi Publishing Ltd
Union House, 111 New Union Street
Coventry CV1 2NT

www.tbjservantofgod.com

Printed in Great Britain by Charlesworth Press, Wakefield.

(20 April 2021)

" *I have read this book from A to Z.
I enjoyed it.
A very interesting book does not need
much time to read.
There is nothing outside me about this
book. It is worth reading.* "

COMMENDATION
from **T.B. Joshua**

CONTENTS

PREFACE

T.B. Joshua recorded the commendation for **TB Joshua - Servant of God** on video on 20 April 2021 at The SCOAN Prayer Mountain, the place where he spent so much of his time seeking God in prayer.

A few weeks later on 5 June 2021, he entered the Prayer Garden and addressed those gathered waiting for him and the wider Emmanuel TV viewers with what was to be his final exhortation,

> I want to thank you for your time and for the heart you have for Jesus.

> Time for everything - a time to come here and a time to return home after service.

He encouraged everyone, quoting the book of Matthew 26:41, *"Watch and pray".*

Leaving the Prayer Garden, T.B. Joshua, aged 57, was then swiftly called home to be with the Lord.

There were accounts of angelic visitations seen in the Prayer Garden that afternoon from those present.

He finished the race well and his earthly assignment was complete.

As news of his passing hurtled around the digitally interconnected globe, tributes began to pour in from all countries and languages, from those who had had the privilege to meet him personally as well as the many who had only met him through the medium of Emmanuel TV.

Tributes came from Presidential Offices, including from the current President of Nigeria, former Presidents, Governors of States in Nigeria as well as government officials from other nations, prominent musicians and actors, journalists, and sportsmen.

Across the continent of Africa, other sitting Presidents including those of South Sudan and Liberia would formally recognise his achievements as an international peacemaker and note that he was a loss to Christendom worldwide, and Africa in particular.

Countless individuals would reflect on how he taught them how to love, how to forgive, and the importance of making the Holy Bible (the Word of God) the standard for their lives. As one viewer from Russia commented, "God made a spiritual revolution through His vessel Prophet T.B. Joshua, changing the world of Christians in their minds and hearts."

T.B. Joshua left a legacy of service and sacrifice to God's kingdom that is living for generations yet unborn. In his own words,

"One life for Christ is all we have; one life for Christ is so dear."

THIS IS IT!

We stood in the large indoor arena with mouths open wide in wonder. We were seeing a scene as if from the Bible, from the Gospels, in front of our eyes. This was no film; this was real.

"In the mighty name of Jesus Christ!"

People all over the auditorium started to react as the prayer of authority was spoken. Those oppressed by negative and satanic spirits could

Mass Prayer in Singapore

not escape; the darkness inside them was exposed and evident for all to see. People screamed and rolled their eyes, falling on the floor, writhing. Those with crutches and in wheelchairs rose as the prayer of faith continued. They walked, their strength increasing with each step.

"Those of you who have little faith, I will pray for you that your faith will be enough", was the echoing prayer. It was a moment of the divine. It was like seeing Jesus at work, and from then on, wherever we showed the recording of that event, there would be miracles. For example, years later, in a back street gospel meeting in inner-city Lahore, Pakistan, with the video projected onto a screen across the street, the same scene was unfolding, and a woman's blind eye opened.

Fast forward some years to a later event held in the largest football stadium in Latin America with its steep high sides; everywhere one looked, there were people from all walks of life experiencing instant miracles as the prayer reverberated throughout the arena. They were neither asked

Crusade with T.B. Joshua in Mexico

to pay anything to enter the mighty stadium nor expected to buy any merchandise. As they witnessed the supernatural work of God and the effect of the 'mass prayer' all around the stadium, there came the spontaneous chanting of *Cristo Vive*, Christ lives.

The scenes were from the National Indoor Stadium in Singapore in 2006 and the Aztec Stadium in Mexico City in 2015, and the pastor praying was a man called T.B. Joshua.

Who is this Jesus in whose mighty name the prayer was offered with the result of seeing the afflicted healed and the oppressed set free? He is the Son of God, the One who shed His blood on the cross for our sins and by whose wounds we are healed.

T.B. Joshua in 2003

Who was this man T.B. Joshua who was proclaiming the word and authority of Jesus Christ? Where did the power come from to make such a dramatic impact without hype, without hysteria?

Why were we present, a conservative British professional middle-aged couple from a quintessential English Cathedral city? How did we come to be involved with this controversial move of God?

GOD'S UNFOLDING PURPOSE

"Many are the plans in a person's heart, but it is the Lord's purpose that prevails." (Proverbs 19:21, NIV)

> "When God Almighty is executing His plan in our lives, He also designs and arranges events which continue to unfold until His purpose is revealed in our lives."[1]

A 'golden thread' of God's purpose was to be seen woven through our life histories. Many years earlier, before we had met each other, we would have our experience of the reality of Jesus in the same month of the same year (May 1973), although our paths would not cross for a further five years. This would then start us on a journey together to our divine destiny and our connection with T.B. Joshua.

Having attended many conferences, meetings and large Christian gatherings across the world, having seen the development of Christian videos and different aids for the Gospel such as the Alpha Course, and having read hundreds of books, now it was 'time'. It was time for our prayers to be answered in a way and manner we did not expect. This would take us on a journey, both inward and outward, that would cause us to see the name of Jesus glorified and propel us into the future God had prepared for us.

Both our lives were already fully occupied. With his burgeoning career in the regulatory and engineering side of independent television broadcasting, Gary was also a 'lay preacher' in our local church. Fiona was involved with charity and church work, looking after family and having an 'open house' for a varied selection of house guests. Our children, who were still studying, also had their lives deeply impacted and began their individual journeys towards their destinies.

During the 1990s, the local reputation of Prophet T.B. Joshua's powerful healing and deliverance ministry had grown, first through

---

1   This is a 'quotable quote' from T.B. Joshua. In the remainder of the book, such quotes are identified by use of similar indentation.

word of mouth and then through video clips shown on local Nigerian TV stations.

One video clip featured a man with a terrible ulcer wound deep within his buttocks (buttocks cancer), unable to sit or even eat properly. His situation deteriorated, and he was 'dumped' at the side of the road. A kind 'good samaritan' found a way to bring him to T.B. Joshua's church, known as The Synagogue, Church Of All Nations (SCOAN). There he received the prayer of faith that introduced him to the Healer, Jesus Christ. As T.B. Joshua was to repeat,

Man Suffering with Buttocks Cancer

> "I am not the healer. I only know the Healer; His name is Jesus Christ!"

Testimony Following His Miraculous Healing

Under the influence of the Holy Spirit, after prayer, the wound miraculously healed. The man gave his testimony before a room of Western inquirers, and the story was included in a 'Divine Miracles 5' compilation on VHS tape. Enthusiastic visitors to the church took home copies to share around.

Thus the news about what God was doing in the life of Prophet T.B. Joshua filtered into Europe via South African pastors visiting The Netherlands and thence to our small quiet city of Winchester in England. A pastor we knew, who had visited The SCOAN more than once, was part of our church relational network. She took a friend from our little church to visit. He brought back some videos, including 'Divine Miracles 5' showing the man healed of buttocks cancer.

In February 2001, after his visit to The SCOAN in Lagos, this friend came into our church meeting, stood up and greeted, 'Emmanuel!'

meaning 'God with us'. Listening intently, something inside of Fiona immediately rose to attention. There was power in that word!

We attended a short monthly leaders' meeting. Our pastor, who was always looking for more, for evidence of 'authentic Christianity', raved about the videos brought back from The SCOAN. At the meeting, where we had so many things we thought were urgent to discuss, he said that we needed to watch these videos because if they were true, they were very significant. He was impacted at a profound level and had realised it was far more important than our leaders' administration meeting.

We watched the shaky camerawork and wondered, but were impacted as much by our pastor's attitude as by the videos themselves. That night, God sowed a seed in our hearts. We thank God for the priority our pastor gave to the mighty miracle and to the Bible teaching on the Holy Spirit from one of the 'Divine Lectures' videos.

We had seen something, and before God, we now had no excuse! We had seen an extraordinary biblical-style miracle recorded on video, something that had demonstrated that,

> "The age of miracles has not passed. The Miracle Worker is still alive - His name is Jesus Christ!"

In retrospect, this was God's answer to our prayers - it pointed to an actual (not theoretical or aspirational) possibility for the fulfilment of our dreams of seeing the name of Jesus glorified in revival.

> "Your greatest opportunities and challenges come unannounced."

EXPERIENCING THE SCOAN

GARY'S FIRST VISIT

The church bus from the airport rocked along unmade-up roads and sometimes, as if to render the journey more exciting, began to move across to the wrong side of the road in full face of the traffic. The driver treated this

Local Lagos Scene in 2001

with casual nonchalance, all in a day's work.

This was my initial visit to Nigeria and The SCOAN, and even though my neighbour on the plane had been a lady trying to warn me not to visit there, I was determined to keep an open mind.

Passing many churches and mosques on the way, seeing the mass of people on the streets that are part of Lagos life, we arrived at the church.

The altar area was where people went to pray, and it was culturally different from the modern Western Protestant churches I was more familiar with, where the emphasis tends to be on the worship space.

The SCOAN Altar in 2001

Dormitory sleeping and different food were part of the package, but as I sat in the warm sanctuary with my Bible, there were two questions in my mind. I had observed to my critical neighbour on the plane that I would be looking for whether the name of Jesus was lifted up and the attitude towards sin. These turned out to be two of the most noteworthy features of the visit. The name of Jesus was much more central than I had ever seen before, and the phrase "sin no more" was not only a motto but reflected an authentic commitment.

The public confession of sin had a great impact on me. One of my fellow group members was a former drug addict who had been drawn into a paramilitary group in Northern Ireland. His deliverance from evil spirits during the service at The SCOAN was dramatic, and his confession hair-raising. Still, something struck me deeply from the standard introduction that was given by one of the evangelists with every confession. As he spoke the words, "Only God Almighty can determine whether one sin is greater than another", my heart was pierced. What about my own, more 'private' sin? Who was to say what I would have done if I had been handed the lot in life that this brother had received, or what he would have done if he had been handed mine?

The Holy Spirit had convicted me of being hypocritical and having become 'religious'. Later, during a personal meeting with Prophet T.B. Joshua, he jotted down some notes in an unknown language and then handed over a scripture promise for meditation. I recall the words of that promise - Psalm 32:5, "He forgave the guilt of my sin" - supernaturally burning inside my heart while I was subsequently repenting at the altar.

Getting back to our peaceful English countryside with green grass and Friesian cows and to all the trappings of middle-class life in a developed country in peacetime was a stark contrast to what I had seen. I had seen the name of Jesus lifted high, I had seen the mighty hand of God at work, and I had rediscovered my 'first love' for Jesus Christ.

FIONA'S FIRST VISIT

Fiona, waiting at home, takes up the story.

I received a call from the airport. "This is it - this is what we have been praying for - healing, deliverance, breakthrough, authority over evil spirits, a love for the Word of God and most of all, a true hatred for sin."

Now it was my turn. Some weeks later, shortly after the world was shaken by the 9/11 terrorist attack, and with some trepidation, I boarded the plane to this new continent. Sharing a dormitory with a group of ebullient Australians, watching the healing and teaching videos until my behind ached, and experiencing the exposure to the anointing of the Holy Spirit led to a challenging, uncomfortable and exhilarating time. I developed a great awareness of sin, where I ended up repenting of my sin and hardness of heart.

Soldier Receives Healing at The SCOAN in 2001

On the prayer line, during the prayer, a warmth came over my neck, and I realised I was healed. As a 19-year-old student nurse, I had suffered a nursing injury that caused back and neck pain and required medication and sometimes a neck support collar. For many years, I also suffered from intermittent insomnia, sometimes only sleeping for two hours before getting the children ready for school. All that was to become a thing of the past.

With a revival-level of awareness of sin burning again in my heart, I waited to enter the small office for my short appointment with T.B. Joshua. I saw him with my eyes, but I didn't 'see' him. The awareness of God was something once

Crowds Outside The SCOAN in 2001

experienced, never forgotten. It reminded me of the great day when as a 17-year-old, I had responded to a Gospel invitation (an altar call) in a formal Baptist church. When the pastor came to shake my hand, I did not see him; instead, I saw a vision of Jesus smiling at me.

This was the same awareness but more profound, hard to explain because no words were spoken. I saw an apostle in the mould of the Bible, one doing the 'greater works' that Jesus said all who believe in Him would do. I was able to see something of the ability of Jesus within him.

> "Jesus Christ described the Holy Spirit as rivers of Living Water, which would flow from the innermost being of believers to meet the needs of others."

That day, I saw this in action. On the plane home, there were only two songs that had been sung at The Synagogue in my mind:

My lifetime, I will give God my lifetime. If I give God my lifetime, He will take care of me. He will never never let me down; I will give God my lifetime.

Who is like my Jesus, who is like my Lord?

As Gary picked me up from Heathrow airport, we were in one spirit and from then on, life would never be the same again. This Bible verse was ringing in my mind,

"But blessed are your eyes for they see, and your ears for they hear; for assuredly, I say to you that many prophets and righteous men desired to see what you see, and did not see it, and to hear what you hear, and did not hear it." (Matthew 13:16-17)

Indeed we were conscious of that blessing.

THE MILLENNIUM

Over the 1999 crossover to the new Millennium, before we had heard the name T.B. Joshua, we had taken our family abroad to a celebration church service in Toronto, Canada and a subsequent three-day Bible-teaching school. On New Year's Day 2000 at the Bible school, at one of the seminars, Guy Chevreau spoke concerning revival and said three things we could not forget:

1. It won't look like you think.

2. There is more going on in the heavenly realms than you can presently imagine.

3. Fulfilment of all you are praying for will take more laying down of your life than most of you are presently comfortable with.

It was just six months later that we first discovered what God was doing through the life of His servant T.B. Joshua. How true we found those simple statements to be.

Several years later, we had the opportunity to meet Guy Chevreau when he was speaking at a church in England and were able to tell him personally how important that message had been to us.

CHRISTIANITY IS NOT A RELIGION

"How do you behave at home, at the market?" With a warm yet serious countenance, the man of God was addressing the congregation.

The sermon about Christlikeness from one of our early visits spoke directly to all of us who were listening. Christianity is not a religion but a relationship with Jesus Christ that should impact the way we live.

T.B. Joshua Preaching in 2002

"Many are Christians by profession and not such in heart. For the deeds generated from the thoughts in the inner room reveal another god, something, someone we have placed above God."

From the early days of having first believed in Jesus, when we read the Bible as if our lives depended on it and had a simpler faith, we had become more 'professional'. We knew the correct language and how to prepare well for various 'Christian' activities, but were our hearts growing closer to God or farther away?

"The main thing about Christianity is not the work we do but the relationship we maintain and the atmosphere produced by that relationship."

It may be possible to impress people by carefully prepared behaviour, but the 'real self' underneath is the one in which God is interested. As T.B. Joshua put it in a more recent message,

"What you do in secret is what will answer you in the open. There is no shortcut to spiritual maturity. We are made spiritual by living in the Word and by the Word living in us."

We also became aware that our belief about salvation was in danger of drifting into something conceptual rather than practical. But as T.B. Joshua says,

"Only your character can testify to the genuineness of your confession of Christ".

We must not only confess with the mouth but believe in the heart, and that belief in the heart is expressed in our character and the small things we do daily, not in mental assent to correct doctrine or facts about Jesus. The new birth is not something purely mystical that we can claim by confession and mental assent alone; it results from the actual practical work of the Holy Spirit to bring about change.

We had read the books and believed we understood the theology about this, but it was the clarity of God's Word and the demonstration of God's Spirit through the ministry of Prophet T.B. Joshua that pierced our hearts with this truth.

John Fletcher, a close associate of John Wesley in the 18th century in England, was dealing with a similar drift into 'religion' when he wrote, with his customary candour,

> If our unregenerate hearers get orthodox ideas about the way of salvation in their heads, evangelical phrases concerning Jesus' love in their mouths, and a warm zeal for our party and favourite forms in their hearts; without any more ado, we

Rev. John W. Fletcher (1729-1785)

> help them to rank themselves among the children of God. But, alas! This self adoption into the family of Christ will no more pass in heaven than self imputation of Christ's righteousness. The work of the Spirit will stand there, and that alone.[2]

PRACTICAL CHRISTIANITY

> "It is not all up to God, and it is certainly not all up to us; It takes God's ability and our willingness to bring about salvation."

This quote from T.B. Joshua reflects the healthy balance between grace and works that is the foundation for 'practical' Christianity. It has been the hallmark of effective believers through the ages. Back in the 17th century, for example, Bishop Ezekiel Hopkins (1634-1690) said essentially the same thing in his sermon on Practical Christianity,

---

2   Fletcher, J. W. (1771). *A second check to antinomianism....* W. Strahan. p. 66

First, So work with that earnestness, constancy and unwearied-ness in well-doing, as if your works alone were able to justify and save you. Secondly, So absolutely rely and depend upon the merits of Jesus Christ for your justification and salvation, as if you had never performed an act of obedience in all your life.[3]

In T.B. Joshua, we saw someone who not only taught this balance more clearly than we had heard before, but his life was a consistent "living letter" of this truth.

DELIVER US FROM EVIL

Another thing that impacted us was the deliverance from evil spirits. This was not pretentious or otherworldly but dealt with the actual source of present evil.

Anger, violence, fear, hatred, continual thoughts of death, pain and torment - every day on our screens or newspapers, we read about deadly deeds inspired by these forces, and we have all experienced them in our own hearts.

In the Lord's Prayer, Jesus Christ teaches us to pray daily, "Deliver us from evil" (Matthew 6:13). Everyone needs deliverance! T.B. Joshua described the daily battle facing believers,

> "There is a constant war between the flesh and the spirit as long as we are in this world. A war is raging in your heart between faith and doubt, humility and pride, hope and despair, peace and anger, patience and impatience, knowledge and ignorance, self-control and greed."

This is not just a figurative war. There are evil spirits of doubt, unfaithfulness, impurity etc., which need to be firmly resisted and denied access to our lives.

Fiona, with her background in the nursing profession, had a

---

3   Hopkins, E. (1701). *The Works of the Right Reverend and Learned Ezekiel Hopkins, Late Lord Bishop of London-Derry in Ireland*. Jonathan Robinson. p. 665

particular perspective,

I learnt that there are also often forces behind physical illness and psychological oppression that we cannot explain naturally. The deliverance in the mass prayer was operating at another level, not working against modern medicine's wonders but adding to them.

We saw that negative forces (spirits) are expelled with a word of authority using the mighty name of Jesus Christ. But we also have a part to play to continue to live victoriously by adopting a lifestyle based on positive thinking, positive action, and positive speaking - by making God's Word the standard for our lives.

CULTURE SHOCK

Our early encounters with The SCOAN were also a culture shock.

One very instructive early video (VHS format) of family reconciliation told the story of a Nigerian man whose girlfriend had become pregnant, and he had abandoned her many years previously. In the church service, a powerful prophetic word from Prophet T.B. Joshua singled out this man who had come to receive prayer for 'breakthrough' in business. He was told he had impregnated a girl in his youth, and he needed to find the girl and take some responsibility for the child. Stunned, the man left the church and went to do all he could to trace the girl, now a single mother. The single mother came with the boy to the church. She was so glad that her son would now have some fatherly and financial care. There was no suggestion that they should marry, but simply that they should take care of the child together so he would have a father. The testimony was very moving and a provocation to those listening that God Almighty sees all. The mother and child were so thankful.

However, back in the UK, Fiona gave the VHS tape to the head of a charity that she volunteered with. This individual watched it through a British cultural lens and commented as though the lady was a single mum in the UK, financially backed by the Welfare State. For her, the main issue was not practical or financial, but emotional - how might the mother have felt when she saw the child's father again? That was quite eye-opening!

We observed something we also saw in ourselves, a subconscious will to impose our own 'culture' as a norm, to sift everything through the filter of our personal worldview.

T.B. Joshua once commented that he had had to live above his culture; the philosophy of Jesus must supersede our norms and upbringing.

However, this work of God was undoubtedly taking place in a cultural setting we were unfamiliar with. The clash of cultures helped us recognise some areas where we had unconsciously understood the Bible within the limitations of our own experience, values and expectations. Here, we were seeing something different that, being more 'raw', was in many ways closer to the Bible.

For example, it was easy for us to interpret the early church as though it had a management structure, with 'elders' having policy meetings and the apostles in Jerusalem being the top-level of supervision. In contrast, it was more about faith and character. T.B. Joshua was not in the mode of a Western-style manager but undoubtedly a provocation to repentance and faith in Christ.

A particular weakness of our middle-class English culture was an overemphasis on appearances. It felt comfortable to focus on presentation, appearance and making new resolutions instead of keeping faithful until the end. Wanting to change may feel good, but the process of real change is often painful and challenging.

SLOWLY BUT SURELY

The vision was terrific and exciting. We had found what we were searching for! But we realised that to realign our lives was no quick fix. We felt that we needed to 'unlearn' many of the good things we had previously learned because they had become culturally tainted, and we had accepted them at too shallow a level.

We had seen an analogy for this in the upgrading of roads in the UK. When traffic had increased so that the road could no longer cope with the volume, it was common to build a new dual-carriageway (divided highway). Although the direction and destination were the same, the old road was usually set aside, and a completely new road built, designed from the outset for the heavier traffic volumes. The same was true for us - we were not heading in some new direction, but we needed to start again from the beginning.

Through the Bible teaching from T.B. Joshua, we saw that the primary tools we would need were patience, perseverance, and endurance. A sermon we found particularly helpful on this was the second in a series called "Slowly but Surely", given in early 2005.

SLOWLY BUT SURELY - PART 2

Sunday Service, The SCOAN, 13 February 2005

John 5:1-14 – (1-6) – *"After this there was a feast of the Jews, and Jesus went up to Jerusalem. Now there is in Jerusalem by the Sheep Gate a pool, which is called in Hebrew, Bethesda, having five porches. In these lay a great multitude of sick people, blind, lame, paralysed, waiting for the moving of the water. For an angel went down at a certain time into the pool and stirred up the water; then whoever stepped in first, after the stirring of the water, was made well of whatever disease he had. Now a certain man was there who had an infirmity thirty-eight years. When Jesus saw him lying there, and knew that he already had been in that condition a long time, He said to him, 'Do you want to be made well?'"*

There are a lot of lessons for us to learn here about God's time. God's time is the best. There is a need to wait for God's time. There was a man at the pool of Bethesda who was not bothered by how long he had to wait because he believed God. He believed that if only he could dip himself into the water, he would be made whole. While waiting by the side of the pool, many others were healed in his presence, and he must have heard many testimonies. He was lying there with no one to help him, but he was not discouraged because he believed in God's time.

John 5:14 - *"Later Jesus found him at the temple and said to him, 'See, you are well again. Stop sinning or something worse may happen to you.'"*

Here in The Synagogue, you can come for prayer for a particular problem, and after the prayer, the problem is solved. A man without vision will not see beyond that healing. But this man in the Bible saw a reason beyond his healing - the salvation of his soul. That was why Jesus found him in the temple, not at a beer parlour or brothel. The Bible indicates that Jesus re-emphasised the need to maintain his miracle by keeping himself holy. That is why He said to him, "Go and sin no more", i.e. don't do it again!

Jesus saw it as necessary to give this conscious warning. It is common for people when sick, lacking, in want or in trouble to make promises. But the day after, they forget everything - the promises, the zeal they showed at the beginning and the suffering they experienced in the past.

Remember the first time you came with difficulty, trouble or sickness. Remember your promise that you would serve your God with all your substance after you became well. Are you still maintaining that promise? This man at the pool of Bethesda kept to his promise; that was why Jesus found him in the temple. He saw a reason beyond his healing. If you had continued your Christian life the way you began it, your situation would not look like it does today. Because the man had a vision, he kept pressing. The man knew where he was going, so he kept pressing.

Where you are going has to do with your divine future; it has to do with your divine destiny. If where I am going today is telling me that I'm going to be a fisherman, by tomorrow, I'm going to buy a fishing net because with it, I know I will prosper.

Where are you going? Are you going towards your divine destiny? If you are going towards your divine destiny, you will have endurance, perseverance and patience. These are the tools. When you have these tools, you will be able to cope. But a man without vision is a man without patience.

A good example is Joseph, the son of Jacob. Consider the road to his divine destiny: From the dry pit to slavery in the house of Potiphar, and then from prison to the throne. It was because he had a vision that he could bear the pain in the dry pit. It was because he had a vision that he could handle the temptation of the wife of Potiphar. It was because he had a vision that he was able to endure the condition of the prison. Each time Joseph found himself in a place which was contrary to his vision, he would say to himself, 'I know where I belong – Not here! This is not God's promise!' This imparted a strength to endure his present condition.

Remember, our trouble becomes easier to handle when we know that it will not last long. Joseph knew that whatever trouble he was going through would be for a short time. The road to your divine destiny, the road to your divine future is not just a bed of roses. You are going to encounter scorpions, snakes, thorns – just name it! That is why you must have endurance. That is why you must have patience. That is why you must have perseverance. When you don't know where you are going, you can't endure; you can't be patient.

Many of you here have God's promise, but you lack patience, perseverance, and endurance. This is a message you should follow up on if you want to succeed in life. If you have a vision, you have where you are going and where you are going has to do with your divine destiny.

When you have a vision, you have boldness; you have confidence. But a man without vision is a man without patience, without perseverance, without endurance. When you have a vision, even when somebody slaps you, you will turn the other cheek if that will allow you to get to your goal.

LIFE AFTER LIFE

"Ekaaro!" Smiling, the ladies from the village greeted Madam Folarin Aisha Adesiji Balogun, mother of T.B. Joshua, in Yoruba on the special day of the naming ceremony in June 1963.

In colourful dresses and carrying large pots of fragrant rice, the ladies started to prepare for the celebration.

"Madam, you must be very thankful to God for your safe delivery. Your little son, what has God Almighty in store for him?" "Yes, he is well, and look at him sleeping peacefully on the mat!" was the happy reply.

The Roof that was Pierced by the Large Piece of Rock

Nearby, the Water Corporation contractors were blasting rocks to make way for their pipes.

All was nearly ready for the naming ceremony, when without warning, a large piece of rock flew from where they were blasting, pierced the roof where people were celebrating and landed where the special little one was placed. But it missed the baby, narrowly. Nobody saw the little one being carried to another part of the room. They only saw that the baby (just seven days old) had shifted and was crying with vigour. But the miracle: he was otherwise unharmed. What was going on in the spiritual world? Only time would tell!

As the screaming subsided and those present were rejoicing, "The baby is safe!"
suddenly, there was more commotion.
Madam Folarin, the mother of the little
Balogun Francis (Joshua to be), was seen
slumped on the ground; efforts to revive
her failed; she was in a deep faint.

An Eyewitness Holds the
Actual Piece of Rock.

"Let us get her to the hospital!" All the neighbours rallied round, the
conveyance for such emergencies was requested, and with someone
carrying the yet unnamed baby, everyone left for the hospital. The
rice was left to spoil.

What had happened? God Almighty had performed a miracle, and
as word went around the village, people were commenting, "We
must watch this child; surely it is God who first protected him in
the womb and now has protected him from death and injury."

T.B. JOSHUA'S BIRTH AND CHILDHOOD

Arigidi in Ondo State, Nigeria

In a rural community called Aridigi
in Ondo State a century ago, there
was an unusual prophecy being
talked about. Balogun Okoorun, a
warrior and farmer, prophesied that
from that rustic community would
emerge a man who would be powerful, famous and have great followers.

Temitope Balogun (later to be called Joshua) was born on 12 June
1963. His father was Pa Kolawole Balogun from Imo quarters, and
his mother, Madam Folarin Aisha Adesiji Balogun from Osin quarters. He was to be the last child.

The history of his time in the womb was to be much discussed. The
baby was quiet in the womb. During the last three months before
the expected delivery, when a good amount of kicking was expected,

there was complete quiet from the in-utero Joshua-to-be. This resulted in a lengthy hospital stay. There were frequent discussions about the possibility of delivery by cesarean section (even now, an expensive, risky procedure in more rural parts of Nigeria).

T.B. Joshua's Childhood Home

His mother recalled that she was lying down on the bed in the hospital, and a pastor walked in and said that she should not be operated on, that God was busy preparing the child. So he advised her to go home, warning that an operation would not be successful. The same message was given to the Doctor.

So, she left the hospital after three months and went back home again to continue the waiting. Eventually, one night, after the 14th month of pregnancy, the baby boy was delivered without an operation. Everyone rejoiced, but the naming ceremony never happened because of the 'flying stone' incident recounted at the beginning of this chapter.

When the baby was finally named, he was given many names, although the one favoured by him and his parents was Temitope, meaning, 'What You (God) have done for me is worthy of thanks'.

Pa Kolawole Balogun, Father of T.B. Joshua

Brought up in a Christian home, his father, whilst still alive, was a farmer and also the secretary to St. Stephen's church in the village. Pa Kolawole died when T.B. Joshua was a small boy. As an early memory, he recalls his father taking him along to the church when he went to work there.

Early signs of spiritual zeal marked his years in Primary School in the village. His favourite subject was Bible Knowledge, or 'BK', and he loved to read the scriptures. Already at that age, he would be reading through the entire Bible regularly and teaching others.

It was there that he gained the nickname 'Small Pastor' and would lead the Student Christian Fellowship.

Saint Stephen's Primary School, Arigidi

One particular incident from those early days was remembered. This was when a madman came to the school with a cutlass. The pupils and teachers were all running around, and no one wanted to go near him. However, the 'small pastor' confidently approached the madman and commanded him to hand over the cutlass in Jesus' name, which he did.

T.B. Joshua After Completing Primary School

Therefore, one could infer that the ministry of T.B. Joshua started from St. Stephen's Primary School, where he collected the cutlass from the madman and started leading the Scripture Union, teaching the Bible and praying for many people. He states that this was where his awareness of God's presence started, and it continued from there. Indeed, "Everything big starts little".

MOVING TO LAGOS

Although he did well at Primary School, his secondary school experience was not to be so straightforward. Indeed it was compounded with many difficulties.

Financial issues in the family meant the fees were not affordable. Although he managed to gain late entry into a Muslim College, Ansar-Ud-deen Grammar School in Ikare near his hometown, there were challenges.

T.B. Joshua Aged 17

Carrying the Bible openly was forbidden, and the small group of Christian believers, with him as leader, would meet in secret to read the Bible. Eventually, he would leave and return home, not continuing any formal education for a while.

Considering how to earn a living to help fund any further education, he decided to move to Lagos. Sleeping on top of a Cassava truck, he hitch-hiked a four-day ride to Lagos and was dropped at Mile 12, home to an enormous international fruit and vegetable market.

Finding a temporary job washing the dirty feet of the market customers, he heard his local dialect being spoken. Interrupting the women talking, they helped him trace his sister, who had moved to Lagos. For a time, he was able to stay with her in Egbe.

Soon, however, unwilling to be a burden to her, he moved on and found a job on a poultry farm carrying chicken dung. He worked at this job for a year, and during that time, he could not get rid of the smell from his body however much soap he used, and often flies would be hovering around him.

T.B. Joshua Aged 20 Even many years later, T.B. Joshua was never to forget what it was like to work day after day in a low-paid, somewhat degrading job that even local Nigerians were unwilling to undertake.

At the same time, he tried to further his education by enrolling in different evening schools. Again, financing himself would always prove a problem as he needed to work full-time to pay for his rent and food.

When he did manage to settle at a school for a while, he was noted as being good at athletics. During this challenging period in his life, he was also teaching children from the Bible.

Efforts to finally move on in the National educational system of Nigeria ended in failure four times. He enrolled for the examinations of JAMB (Joint Admission and Matriculation Board), but for different reasons, such as having an accident on the way to the exam venue and sometimes forgetting vital documents, his efforts were frustrated.

Some were puzzled by this conundrum, but thankfully his mother, a woman of faith, saw it as something God was involved in - a 'stopping interval' on the journey to his destiny.

Nowhere was this more evident than a potentially deeply disappointing experience in trying to enlist in the Nigerian army.

This time he passed the entrance examination for the Nigerian Defence Academy, Kaduna and was invited for an interview. Perhaps this time, success was beckoning? However, the train on which he was travelling from Lagos to Kaduna developed serious faults, breaking down and leaving all the passengers for six long days in the 'bush' in Kwara State with little food. He missed the interview as he lacked the financial means to arrange any other way of getting there.

T.B. Joshua would later reflect, "Who knows what would have happened if I had successfully attended that interview? I felt very bitter that I had missed another chance of making it in life."

Returning to the village, the words spoken to him by his mother would comfort him in his season of enduring a 'dry pit', as did Joseph in the well-known account in Genesis.

> My son, do not mind the seeming appearance of things as of today. If I am ever confident of any child, you are that child. Do not be afraid of what the future holds for you because I know if anyone is destined to fail, you are not the one. So, be patient, and you will see what God would do in your life. I am so sure of your future breakthrough, considering the strength of the predictions and prophecies about you even before you were born. I cannot forget so easily what I experienced when I was pregnant with you, and I know God cannot lie. Whatever you may be going through today, my son, take it as a temporary setback meant to prepare you for the challenges ahead. Don't forget your name is 'Temitope' and, by the grace of God, the

whole world shall have the cause to thank God for your sake.[4]

Indeed that word of faith was to come to pass. Years later, his Bible teaching about Joseph on Emmanuel TV would encourage thousands.

The 'dry pit' is where you can see no way out of the situation, no source of supply, but as Joseph of old did not give way to bitterness and offence, neither did Temitope Balogun Joshua. Later he was to comment,

> In my spiritual walk with God, I have experienced both good and hard times. Who knows what would have happened if those temporary stops did not come at intervals. Remember, when God is executing His plan in our lives, He also designs and arranges events that continue to unfold until His purpose is revealed. The ups and downs in my education were part of the events that revealed the purpose of God in my life. Remember, the man who is poor is not the man that has no money, but one without a dream.[4]

He has frequently acknowledged his mother's positive example in his sermons, referring, for instance, to her tireless cleaning in the church while praying that God would clean her heart as she was cleaning His house. He also attributed the following quote to her, which positively impacted his life:

> "When times are stable, and the sea is calm and secure, no one is really tested."

Years later, whilst he was in The Bahamas, where he was received by the country's Governor-General, he was informed of his mother's last illness. She subsequently passed away before he could return to Nigeria.[5]

T.B. Joshua with a Picture of His Mother

---

4   *My Stopping Interval*, SCOAN Blog, 5 October 2009
5   *Untold Story Of A Mystery - Prophet TB Joshua*, The Sun (Nigeria), 5 Apr 2009

DIVINE CALLING

The year was 1987, and following his years in Lagos, the Holy Spirit instructed T.B. Joshua to undertake a prolonged time of seeking the face of God on a mountain near his hometown of Arigidi. There, he fasted and prayed for 40 days and 40 nights. He wrote that in a heavenly vision, he received divine anointing and a covenant from God to start his ministry:

LIFE AFTER LIFE

I was in a trance for three consecutive days, then I saw a hand that pointed a Bible to my heart, and the Bible entered my

Praying on the Mountain

heart, and my former heart seemed to immerse with the Bible immediately. Then the awareness came, and I saw the apostles and prophets of old with someone whose head I could not see because He was tall to the heaven and suspended, which I believe was our Lord, Jesus Christ, sitting in their midst. I also saw myself in their midst. After a while, I saw a hand of the same tall man; I could not behold His face, which was glittering with an unimaginable light, tall to the high heavens and suspended in the air. But other apostles, I could see their faces, particularly Apostles Peter and Paul, Prophets Moses, Elijah and others. Their names were boldly written on their chests.

I heard a voice saying, 'I am your God; I am giving you a divine commission to go and carry out the work of the Heavenly Father'. At the same time, the same hand of the tall man gave me a small cross and a big Bible, bigger than the one that entered my heart with a promise that as I keep pressing in His time and name, I would be given a bigger cross but if I fail the opposite would occur. I also heard the voice of the same tall man (I could not see His head), saying, 'I am the Lord your God who was and who is – Jesus Christ', giving orders to all the apostles and prophets. The same voice said to me, 'I would show you the wonderful ways I would reveal myself through you, in teaching, preaching, miracles, signs and wonders for the salvation of souls'.

Since then, I have been receiving in my vision, every year according to my faithfulness to God, a bigger cross that means to me more responsibilities.

The Bible that entered my heart symbolised Spirit and life (the Holy Spirit). God's Word is Spirit and life. He does nothing without His Word. The Book of Romans 8:16 says that God's Spirit joins Himself to our spirit to declare that we are children of God. The Father gave the Spirit to make us like His Son.

Father, thank You for Your Spirit, fill us with Your love and power, change us into Christ's own image, day by day and hour by hour.

God Himself performs the divine anointing on all who have the wonderful privilege of becoming His children (2 Corinthians 1:21-23 and Luke 24:48-49).[6]

T.B. Joshua on His Return from a 40 Day Fast

THE BEGINNINGS OF THE CHURCH

T.B. Joshua Walking in 1989

As the video documentary, *This Is My Story*, shows, T.B. Joshua's mode of transport in those early years would be walking everywhere. Anywhere he went, children followed him. Those children and their mothers would make up some of the very first church members.

In 1989, he laid the foundation of the first Synagogue church located in Agodo-Egbe, Lagos, Nigeria. He walked joyfully among the first members as he lifted their faith with the Word of God. Here is a transcript of that short, lively sermon:

---

6   *How God Called TB Joshua*, Distance Is Not a Barrier Blog, static page

Hallelujah! Let us be seated. Amen! In fact, I don't know where to start. Amen! My coming to your midst is just to lay a foundation. I am here to lay a foundation, that today we start The Synagogue here! The Synagogue has started here! I have come to launch a good foundation for the church. You should know that this man always says things in proverbs.

All the elders here have been hearing from a young age that Jesus is coming. We have been expecting His coming up until now, and we are still preparing for it. The reason Jesus has not come is because He wants you and me to repent of our sins because He doesn't want

The First Church in 1989

anyone to perish. Have you repented? The reason the coming of Jesus is delayed is because God wants you to repent. Repent from your sin so that you will not perish. By the time Jesus comes, you will not perish; you will inherit the Kingdom of God. Right from your childhood, you have been learning that Jesus will come like a thief in the night. We have been waiting for the coming of Jesus. The reason the coming of Jesus has been delayed is because of you and me. Jesus wants you to repent; he doesn't want you to perish. By the time He comes, he can carry you to eternal life. If Jesus should come and you have not repented, the coming of Jesus in your life has no meaning. In order for the coming of Jesus to have meaning in your life, you need to repent. You have to repent today and accept Jesus. So that when Jesus comes, you can join Him in the Kingdom of God.

So, for me and my house - and I believe you are my house - we will serve Lord. Clap for Jesus! Hallelujah![7]

It wasn't long before the numbers grew to require a new church building, the second church, which was on the same site. However, this simple structure was destroyed during a violent thunderstorm.

---

7 *This Is My Story: TB Joshua Documentary*, TB Joshua Ministries Facebook Post, 2 Nov 2017

The Second Church, Destroyed by a Storm

After the second church building was destroyed, another building was built, this time using wooden planks. The first service was held at the new building of The Synagogue, Church Of All Nations, in 1992.

The third church building also suffered severe damage from flooding. Because of this and the increasing number of worshippers attending the church, the Holy Spirit instructed T.B. Joshua to move to a new location about two miles away.

The Third Church in 1992

Thus, in 1994, the church moved to Ikotun-Egbe, its current location. This was the fourth building of The Synagogue Church of all Nations, the first church building on the new site. It was this building, extended, that we came to when we first visited the church in 2001.

The Fourth Church in 1994

The site of the first three churches is now the site of The SCOAN's Faith Resort Ground, also known as 'Prayer Mountain'.

FALSE ARREST

That period between 1994 and 2001 saw substantial growth in the church's impact and the corresponding persecution. In 1996, T.B. Joshua was even falsely accused of drug dealing and spent 13 days in prison. Here is a news report of a confession made three years later in the church by one of the officers who arrested him in 1996 on the accusation of drug dealing:

> Yusuf Hassan, who hails from Adamawa State, said he worked with the National Drug Law Enforcement Agency when an informant tipped them off that Joshua was dealing drugs within his church premises.

> Storming The Synagogue Church of All Nations in Lagos with 18 "armed" officers and six soldiers, Yusuf recounted how the cleric was arrested and subsequently incarcerated for 13 days.

> "On our way to the office, we asked him that – if he was a man of God, let him disappear," Hassan reminisced, describing how the operatives all taunted the cleric en route to prison.

Falsely Arrested in 1996

> "Our officers destroyed a lot of things while searching for drugs – but we couldn't find anything. On the 13th day, he was released because nothing incriminating was found on him or with him," Yusuf continued.

> However, after Joshua's innocence was established, Hassan revealed that calamity befell all involved in the operation.

> "Among the officers that came to arrest T.B. Joshua, three of them are no longer alive. All 18 officers, except for myself, have been dismissed," he revealed.

> Yusuf himself said he was "on suspension" after a court case landed him in prison for ten months.

> "I want God to deliver me from the part I took in this arrest," he concluded.[8]

Imagine the rumours and gossip that spread due to this incident - a prophet detained in a cell, accused of dealing drugs and harbouring

---

8   *Throwback as NDLEA Officer recounts arrest of TB Joshua for 'dealing in drugs',* The Eagle Online, 23 Sep 2019

weapons. However, his enemies found that not even detention in a cell and false accusations would shake his faith in God. On his first appearance at the church, having just been released, he encouraged the congregation,

> If you say to yourself, 'Why me of all this trouble, persecution, tribulation and all sorts of things?', I want you to think back and ask, 'Why me of all these spiritual blessings in my life?'[9]

A Christian's distinguishing mark is that difficulties, challenges, pressures, and persecution drive them closer to God, not further away.

EMMANUEL TV IS BORN!

In March 2006, a significant birth took place, one that was to change many people's lives for the better; Emmanuel TV was born. However, the emergence of such a powerful means of communication came about in an unusual way.

"Sir," the evangelists crowded into the tiny office, "Our President, he is banning miracles being shown on our TV here in Nigeria, both the local stations and the National broadcaster. They say that from now on, our programmes should only show you preaching. It feels like persecution, Man of God; many people have been watching on these local stations and thanking God for what is happening."

T.B. Joshua himself explained what happened next,

> I removed my programme from all the stations. I went to the prayer mountain, and God said, "I am aware; I want you to discover yourself". God asked me to open a TV channel, and God said, "Emmanuel TV". I changed it by myself to "SCOAN TV". The cloud went dark, and God said, "When you wake up, change the name to Emmanuel TV". I was warned by God. That was how Emmanuel TV started.[10]

In those early days, we remember him declaring publicly that Emmanuel TV would become bigger than The Synagogue, Church Of All

---

9   *This Is My Story: TB Joshua Documentary*
10   *Fear Next!* SCOAN Blog, 31 May 2017

Nations. At the time, it was hard to imagine, but now it is plainly true. The satellite channel is a household name and widely viewed across much of sub-Saharan Africa. By 2021, Emmanuel TV had become the most-watched general Christian channel worldwide on YouTube.

It was indeed evident that,

> "Man's rejection provokes God's direction."

One of the fruits of Emmanuel TV has been to correct some rumours about what happens at The SCOAN. There have been several testimonies where those formerly persecuting and speaking against The SCOAN have, through Emmanuel TV, seen the reality of what is happening and then repented of their previous words and actions.

One notable example took place in the Sunday Service at The SCOAN on 7 April 2013, when a pastor and his wife publicly shared their testimony and confession. As a prominent leader, he had previously preached at national youth rallies that T.B. Joshua was the 'antichrist of our generation'. However, in an ironic twist of fate, the man he had campaigned against and slandered religiously ended up being the one used by God to set his family free from spiritual bondage through deliverance. This was after he had started to watch Emmanuel TV in secret, and what he saw was very different from what he had been told. In his final words of advice, he pleaded with his fellow ministers to find out the truth before rushing to judgement.

THE LIVE SERVICE

Since 2007, the main SCOAN services have been broadcast live on Emmanuel TV. These live services have been, for many around the world, a highlight of the week. Across the world, in different time zones, the excitement builds, "What will happen in the live service today? What will God be doing? Will T.B. Joshua personally take part, and if so, what Bible-teaching message will he bring? Which testimony and life experience will be highlighted?"

The testimonies would offer a window into a person's life and background. Marriage breakups and reconciliation, nothing was 'off limits' so the people of God could learn and be warned by others' experiences.

There have been harrowing cases of older women who were so fearful of being labelled a witch because they could be burned to death. The whole family would be invited to the church and given free accommodation and food so that all the key members would be involved, have their say and hear the wisdom of the man of God. At home in different parts of Nigeria, other family members would be gathering around a TV screen (praying the electricity would not go down), waiting to hear what T.B. Joshua would say. These judgments would save lives, reduce the violence that came from ignorance, and preserve the whole family's dignity.

The live services typically culminated with mass prayer. This acted as a spiritual health check; it set one up for the week ahead.

"Quick, gather round!" People from households across the world would be eagerly waiting for the mass prayer, the 'Prayer for Viewers' part of the live service, and the words "Viewers all over the world, touch your screen". In praying for the viewers, T.B. Joshua would directly address the camera and stretch his hand towards the lens. Frequently, the testimony section would include those who had indeed 'connected by faith' with this prayer and were now eagerly giving glory to God for what He had done.

The SCOAN Sunday service was to develop swiftly into a significant event every week with hundreds visiting from other nations. In Ikotun Egbe, hotels were springing up in the local vicinity and the local economy improved by all the visitors milling around in the streets outside the church. As the number of international visitors to the church grew, the team became experienced in dealing with different cultures. The development of the live service and the substantial turn out of national and international visitors meant that truly one saw The SCOAN living up to its prophetic name as

The Synagogue, Church Of *All Nations*. One could look around and see the scores of flags from different countries on any given Sunday.

A FAMILY MAN

From the earliest days of our involvement with T.B. Joshua, his supportive wife Evelyn was at his side and as a powerful preacher

in her own right. Walking into the Visitors Dining room at The SCOAN, one saw a beautiful picture of her accepting the award of the OFR (Officer of the Order of the Federal Republic of Nigeria) from President Yar'Adua on behalf of her husband.

Mrs Evelyn Joshua with President Yar'Adua

At many international events, adapting graciously to the host country's cultural expectations, she received gifts of flowers or local handmade crafts on the stage. Sometimes, as in the South Korea Crusade of 2016, Prophet T.B. Joshua was to be seen flanked by his whole family standing in line to welcome the Committee in the Hotel Foyer. Their adult daughters, known for excelling in various academic achievements, were often seen accompanying their father on charitable visits to the elderly and being an integral part of the Emmanuel TV event teams.

However, perhaps our most enduring memory of Sister Evelyn is her accompanying her husband stoutly marching along the muddy tracks in the Ecuador Rainforest, clad in wellington boots. With the vehicle stuck in the mud, they were completing the journey on foot to open the school provided by Emmanuel TV after the 2016 earthquake. All captured on camera for the glory of God was the timely provision of a local brother with a horse who helped carry the man of God's wife and another evangelist on the final stretch of the tiring journey.

Love for animals was always part of T.B. Joshua's life, connecting with nature and creation. Birds, antelopes and peacocks roam freely at the 'Prayer Mountain' site in Lagos, also known as the 'Faith Resort Ground'. The animals have even featured in Emmanuel TV cartoon-style productions, 'reflecting on their favourite Bible teaching'.

T.B. Joshua Studying at the Prayer Mountain

THE HOLY BIBLE - AN INTEGRAL PART OF THE STORY

> "The Word of God has the ability to develop a force within our heart called faith."

It is clear from the story of T.B. Joshua's childhood and calling that the Bible had always been a central part of his life and ministry. We have observed over the years that his approach to the Bible is different. He read avidly, but not in an 'academic' way. And his preaching manages to explain what the Bible is getting at in a simple but profound way. The key themes that run through his messages do not reflect a 'systematic' theology but rather an emphasis on characteristics that are important to the heart of God, as revealed through the Bible.

Reading the Bible is itself one of the common themes in his sermons, and it becomes clear that this is not just a matter of reading like one would a textbook or novel, but that the heart attitude of the reader is crucial. We must read the Bible as if our lives depend on it.

Over 250 years ago, John Wesley displayed a similar attitude to reading the Bible. In the preface to his published sermons, he writes,

> I am a creature of a day, passing through life as an arrow

through the air. I am a spirit come from God, and returning to God: Just hovering over the great gulf; till, a few moments hence, I am no more seen; I drop into an unchangeable eternity! I want to know one thing — the way to heaven; how to land safe on that happy shore. God himself has condescended to teach the way: For this very end he came from heaven. He hath written it down in a book. O give me that book! At any price, give me the book of God! ... I meditate thereon with all the attention and earnestness of which my mind is capable.[11]

This is a clear example of an attitude of paying attention to the Word of God as if our life depends on it, which it does!

Read the Word of God as if your life depends on it:

Read it - it has a purifying power (John 15:3).

Read it - it has converting power (1Peter 1:23).

Read it - it has enduring power (Psalm 119:89).

Read it - it has healing power (Psalm 107:20).

Read it - it is a guide to your feet (Psalm 119:105).

Read it - it is so profitable (2 Timothy 3:16-17).

Read it - it is your Spiritual weapon (Ephesians 6:17).

Read it - it keeps you from error and sin (Psalm 119:11).

Read it - it points to life (Proverbs 6:23).

Read it - it rejoices the heart (Psalm 19:8).

Read it - we are commanded to do so (Joshua 1:8).

(T.B. Joshua)

---

11 Wesley, J. (1746). *Sermons on Several Occasions ..; Volume 1.* W. Strahan. Preface

WHO IS LIKE MY JESUS?

" Jesus," she kept praying. "This is my last chance, my last bus stop; please use the man of God to help me, please let my baby be born healthy."

Dressed in an orange cloth dress with matching headscarf, she had come to The SCOAN early in the morning on local transport and waited with the swelling crowd to be seen by the evangelists. Having related her predicament, to her relief, she found herself placed at the Prayer Line section, conscious of her swelling stomach and the baby who was not kicking. What was happening in her womb?

The ever creeping darkness of fear and disappointment tried to infect her thoughts with doubts such as, 'You are not the only pregnant woman here today. Look at all these people waiting for prayer. Why would you be helped?'

Resolutely, she mopped the perspiration from her face with a handkerchief and continued her prayer. "Lord Jesus Christ, let Your mercy and favour speak for me today; You are the Healer, You are the Creator of my baby in the womb. Please use the man of God to rescue me today!"

Suddenly, the wait was over. In the distance, at the bottom of the walkway, where for so many years the prayer line had taken place, she could see action. The team was moving around, cameras were evident, and she strained her eyes. Was it him? "Yes," her neighbour said, "That is T.B. Joshua."

As he moved up the line, stretching his hand to pray and prophesy, the team came ahead and asked those waiting to stand whilst they stood behind the chairs.

He came in sight wearing a beige garment, local style, and fixing his eyes on her, expressed a command. For the rest of her life, she would never forget that sound. It was a command to her baby in the name of Jesus Christ.

Instantly, she felt the water flowing; she was in labour and began instinctively to remove her skirt.

The Baby is Born Instantly on the Prayer Line

The man of God said, "No, no, no! Cover her!" and again, the sound of authority. Immediately her passage opened, her womb opened, everything opened, and on the floor dropped her baby girl with the placenta following.

After that, events became a blur as the experienced helpers took her to the toilet and, checking the placenta was completely delivered, cut the cord, wrapped her miracle baby in a clean cloth and took her away to rest.

We were among the group of visitors who witnessed that unbelievable miracle with our own eyes. The next day, the visitors were treated to a sight of the beautiful, healthy baby and heard the whole story of how she was sick and the baby was not moving in the womb. We marvelled and thanked Jesus.

The little girl thrived and grew. She was to be seen ten years later returning to The SCOAN to give a follow-up testimony and report her excellent school progress.

CHURCH OF ALL NATIONS

The Holy Spirit had directed T.B. Joshua to move to Lagos (the former colonial capital of Nigeria) and set him apart for the Lord's work. He was told to start his ministry and call it *The Synagogue, Church Of All Nations*. To put this into context, Ikotun Egbe is in an underdeveloped area on the outskirts of the sprawling megapolis, where nearly everyone is Nigerian. The promise of a church for all nations in that neighbourhood seemed almost impossible, like Abraham in the Bible being told he would be a father of many nations when his wife was childless and aged 90 (Genesis 17). Furthermore, The Synagogue's beginning, under a tree with a few women and children, was inauspicious. But it had to be. T.B. Joshua often said:

> "Everything big starts little; if something starts big, it calls for concern."

and also,

> "When a vision is from God, there will be a strong desire to make it happen. Even if you cannot see how, you will achieve it. No matter the obstacles on the way to your destination, you will always find ways of building bridges which close the gap from where you are now to your destination." (see Philippians 3:13)

Even before any international visitors came to Ikotun Egbe, the church members all knew the vision that one day the church would be global with visitors from all over the world. We were later to meet someone who had come to study in the UK, who had heard this said frequently during the very early days of the church and had wondered how it could possibly come to pass. But she was also in the church the first day an international visitor appeared, a white pastor from South Africa who had heard about the miracles, and she knew that God was faithful to fulfil His promises.

EARLY GROUP VISITS

In the 1990s, earnest believers in Jesus (primarily from the West and of Protestant persuasion) were ready to travel the world in search of revival, i.e. evidence of the power of God in action. Christian believers, first in South Africa and then in Europe, the US and Asia, began to hear of this man in Nigeria. He lived a simple life in a prayer hut, a righteous man who God was using. People were impressed by what they heard about this humble man of God who spent much time in prayer. It appeared from the evidence that God was using him mightily in signs and wonders.

The power of God was obvious and evident, and did we not all need power? Yes, indeed, but those who visited The SCOAN quickly saw that it is more about righteousness, seeking first the Kingdom of God.

From about 1999, international visitors started coming. The sick received healing, the oppressed were delivered, and there were many testimonies! Following our initial visits in 2001, we began to take friends to experience this great church. The group visits quickly developed, primarily by word of mouth, to include others we had not met before.

There were many different people facilitating group visits to The SCOAN around this time. Visitors were marvelling at what God was doing but also trying to fit it into a 'revival box'. But this was different - a righteous man, a prophet of biblical proportions, a modern Joshua. The miracles and demonstrations of authority over evil spirits, some,

The Synagogue is not about The Synagogue but about a new level of devotion to Jesus Christ

in particular, were visually amazing. This caused a reaction, some marvelling, some sceptical.

Some of those who marvelled tried to copy the externals of what they saw - the style of prayer etc. Others became interested in The Synagogue as a potential model for the way of 'doing church'. But this was missing the point. As we used to tell people before their visit, "The Synagogue is not about The Synagogue but about a new level of devotion to Jesus Christ."

"After my visit to The SCOAN, I feel the presence of the Holy Spirit constantly guiding me and the love of Jesus Christ."
Animesh, USA

Many visitors would come with their shopping list of prayer requests, but the Holy Spirit would heal, deliver, bless as He wills! As the 15th-century German theologian Thomas à Kempis said in his classic book *The Imitation of Christ*, "Homo proponit, sed Deus disponit", or, "Man proposes, but God disposes."

T.B. Joshua explained some of the limitations of a 'shopping list' approach to prayer,

"People think today that healing, miracles, gifts of prophecy and all of God's blessings are wrought at will by the person concerned. That is why when you meet a prophet, you ask for prayer, not minding whether it is the right time or not. We are not used to a prophet."

THE VISIT EXPERIENCE

The vast country of Nigeria is not usually a destination for international tourists. Most people only travelled there for business or because they were Diaspora, to see family. It was often difficult to get visas even with a formal Invitation from the church, a prerequisite to visit.

The visitors were treated as individual guests of T.B. Joshua, and in the early days, there was no charge. As numbers grew, the accommodation would be charged for, incorporating food and transport.

A South African visitor described being at The SCOAN as 'a little piece of Heaven on earth'. Why? Because of a fulfilment of the Lord's Prayer, "Your kingdom come, Your will be done, on earth as it is in heaven". It is a place on earth where God's will is done, and God's Kingdom is advanced.

There was an incredible sense of righteousness and holiness which one experienced when visiting The SCOAN. There, one's desire to read the Bible increased, and one was more aware of sin and the need to change. God was real, and His presence could be felt. Some East-ern European visitors also claimed they saw angels at the church and the Prayer Mountain. Sometimes there were unusual phenomena in photos they took, like the one here taken in 2006 at the church entrance.

The overarching reason for visiting was to pursue God for 'salvation of soul', draw closer to Him, and grow in holiness. The emphasis was entirely on one's spiritual life and personal walk with Jesus Christ, whose name is held in the highest honour at The SCOAN. We found it very refreshing.

We always told potential visitors in our groups that a week at The SCOAN was more akin to a retreat in a monastery than a typical Christian conference, with its pre-planned programme of teaching sessions and minis-try. At any time, the visitors could be called to pray, receive a lecture or even to go to the Prayer Mountain at night.

Fiona at the Prayer Mountain in 2005

The visitors' dining room acted as the 'common room'. Between meals, the visitors would typically be encouraged to get out their Bibles and notebooks and watch a selection of Bible teaching, miracle and deliverance videos. As Emmanuel TV developed, its schedule would take the place of these VHS tapes. The church sanctuary was open 24/7 for private prayer, and many visitors would choose to spend some 'quiet time' there each day. There would also be visits to the Prayer Mountain, live teaching, and sometimes question and answer sessions with T.B. Joshua.

One time, he was talking to the visitors and asked them, "Do you want to know Jesus' direct phone number - the one to call and get an answer, not just to fill the air with loud cries?" We all listened, trying to understand, and he explained very simply - the direct line phone number is 'believe'. That is, when we talk to God, we need to believe He hears us and will answer in His own way and time. We are not just filling the air.

For most visitors, the big highlights were the Sunday service, and in the early days, Wednesday services as well. We would often be invited also to attend Monday Newcomer meetings. The services would typically take all day, and in some cases, they would extend into the night also. All the services continued even in the middle of the major reconstruction project for the new 'cathedral' in 2003.

Construction of the New Church Building in 2003

Many would come to us as group leaders and say, "I want T.B. Joshua to talk to me in the service; I want to discuss my problem with him". We would always have one answer, "You need to go to the top, to talk to his General, his boss - Jesus Christ! He is the one who instructs

T.B. Joshua, who is simply a servant."

Before the service at which they would receive prayer, the visitors were interviewed, and their physical diagnoses were displayed boldly on placards. This was a novel approach for many, but the purpose was to shame satan, the 'evil one'.

After receiving the prayer, some people would feel the urge to 'vomit' or cough and spit out excess saliva, phlegm, or even blood. This was a new phenomenon to many visitors, but later we would discover that it was not confined to any particular culture; it would occur in other countries where T.B. Joshua or his evangelists travelled to pray. The response often indicated a form of deliverance from evil spirits and was frequently accompanied by pain relief or other healing.

Vomiting Poisonous Substances

A sanitation team would arm themselves with gloves, mops, disinfectant, buckets, and clean sand in the firm expectation that God's power would manifest in such ways; later, there would be sanitised trays at events. At The SCOAN, strong middle-aged ladies would typically take this role, beautifully dressed with their starched colourful local headgear.

The person vomiting would be encouraged to kneel and not to lie on their back for safety reasons. There was vigilant observation, and once all was complete, the person would be offered fresh tissues to wipe their mouth and a reassuring arm to help them sit back on their chair.

The authority over evil spirits during the services was at a level like we read about in the Book of Acts. There was a season when the 'ogbanjes' (demonised individuals) would be spiritually 'arrested' by prayer. Without a human touch, their legs would lock themselves in a crossed position, and they would be cared for with Bible teaching and food and shelter for a few days, usually until the next service.

At this point, they would be lined up next to the SCOAN altar, give their confession and then receive deliverance and be sent on their way with encouragement to live for Jesus.

Public confession, often X-rated in content, was an integral part of the major deliverance cases; it was how people could learn and be warned about falling into the same trap. Some of the stories could only be described as 'hair-raising' and certainly not suitable for sensitive ears. Still, they were a 'raw' education for many who had lived a sheltered life.

"Prior to my deliverance at The SCOAN, I used to place so much value on worldly things, but now I've found a purpose to life and beyond."
Lerato, Germany

Over the years, different examples would provide insights into the spiritual world. There were stories of watching over dead bodies for months, all manner of ways that evil spirits could impact the human body and soul, and detailed descriptions of temptations that drew people away from settled family life into pornography addiction, fornication, violence, adultery or fraud. As internet access spread more widely over the vast continent of Africa through 'smartphone' technology, there was a season when there was a specific focus in deliverance and confession on 'internet cases'.

Meeting the Man of God

For over 25 years, T.B. Joshua tried to see, individually, each visitor - old and young, rich and poor, educated and uneducated, believer and unbeliever, Christians, those from other faiths or no faith. This encounter was the one thing every international visitor eagerly anticipated. It was a marathon for the SCOAN team to arrange for every single visitor to see the man of God and still get them to the airport on time. It was a holy assignment in which the evangelist team excelled.

One waited with a beating heart on the chairs outside the small office. On entering, whether one met 'Mr' or 'Prophet' T.B. Joshua appeared to depend on how one had used the time at The SCOAN and one's openness to God. Some saw 'Mr' only and received a welcome and a handshake and a bag of gifts, e.g. videos, sermon notes, T-shirts or Anointed Stickers. Others saw a prophet, a true believer from whose belly was flowing the Living Water, the Holy Spirit, to meet their needs by anointed prophecy and prayer. But on the outside, it looked the same.

"When you are close to the man of God, you feel the fear of God, a tremulous atmosphere and reverence. And it definitely leads you to a deeper delight and the holy fear of God."

Julia, Ukraine

Profoundly reassured that Christianity was not a religion but a relationship with Jesus, and the Acts of the Apostles were still happening today, with our hearts filled with the joy of God, there would be warm good-byes from the team, and we would get on the bus to go to the airport.

Such was the case of a certain elderly British man.

A friend, a pastor, was worried about his father, who was a convinced unbeliever. He took his father, who had severe cataracts, on one of the visits to The SCOAN. What happened was amazing! This man in his late 80s was well looked after but not placed on the prayer line. In the office with his son, Prophet T.B. Joshua gave him a personal word of knowledge, something nobody knew, not even his son. The next day on the plane home, the father cried and confessed to his son, who then led him in a prayer of commitment to Jesus Christ. From that day on, the father was different, wanting to be taught the Scriptures. Not much later, he would pass away, and Fiona attended the joy-filled funeral where the pastor rejoiced, stating his belief that his father was now in heaven.

Our faith is more precious than gold. The God we serve is beyond the trials and the joys of this life; only faith pleases God.

FAITH IN ACTION

In one visitors' teaching session, T.B. Joshua encouraged us, with a fatherly smile, "You are looking for healing, but if you go to the market, you understand you can't buy a $5 garment with only $2. In the same way, your capacity to believe needs to increase for what you are asking for. Faith is a Heavenly currency that purchases Heavenly things. The amount of faith you have is the amount of Heavenly resources you receive." This was a straight-forward message we could all understand. So the question was, "How do we increase our capacity to believe?" The answer came swiftly,

> "Your capacity to believe can increase or decrease depending on how much you feed your soul with the Word of God, the Holy Bible."

We also learnt that faith must be tested in order to become established in our hearts and grow.

"The trip to The SCOAN changed my life. I was freed from the spirit of fear. I have now learned to think in a new way, and my spiritual life has grown."
Veronika, Estonia

There were times when a person's faith was tested mightily in the same way as the demonised daughter's mother, who both Jesus and his disciples famously ignored.

"A Canaanite woman from that vicinity came to him, crying out, 'Lord, Son of David, have mercy on me! My daughter is demon-possessed and suffering terribly.'

Jesus did not answer a word. So his disciples came to him and urged him, 'Send her away, for she keeps crying out after us.'" (Matthew 15:22-23, NIV)

Jesus was testing her faith. In the end, the praise that Jesus bestowed upon this woman is a message and encouragement to all.

"Woman, you have great faith!" (Matthew 15:28, NIV)

This occasion is memorable in many ways, and we have seen it echoed in T.B. Joshua, as he publicly commends humble village folk for their rock-solid belief in the redemptive power of Jesus.

A SCOAN Sunday Service in 2009

Some visitors stepped onto The SCOAN site, took a deep breath, and knew in their heart that they had arrived in the arena of liberty. That kind of faith received from God. Whether or not the person was placed on any prayer line, whether they stayed in the church accommodation or a nearby local hotel, whether anyone laid hands on them in prayer or not, did not matter very much. Whether their needy loved ones were present with them or whether they had only brought their pictures was not a significant concern. They had the Heavenly currency of faith in Jesus Christ, our mediator and advocate. Such people would often give testimony the following week, making it clear that there are no methods or magic steps to follow.

Equally, a person could be part of a group, be placed for prayer on the prayer line and receive from God, but then swiftly lose the blessing on returning home. We have an essential role to play in maintaining our blessing!

Everything big starts little; our trust in God as the Healer needs to be exercised in the small challenges of daily life. As any runner knows, one cannot just run a marathon if one cannot run 5 km.

Sometimes visitors would be asked to bring a picture of their sick relative and stand in proxy for them. For those who could receive this in faith, they saw the visit as a time to draw close to God and to place their loved ones in His mighty hands. Prophet T.B. Joshua might well receive from God a personal prophecy or Word of knowledge for the person in such cases. God responds to our faith, not our desperation.

Other visitors learned through having to wait that indeed, "God's time is the best". We remember well one Russian lady, who did not receive confirmation of her request to visit The SCOAN and wondered why. Several months passed, and she happily joined another group visit later and received prayer for her and her family in the Sunday service. The following day, we met her at the breakfast table, rushing up and down to find the translator.

> *"I went to The SCOAN as a religious person, and I came back home as a new person, a new creation in Christ."*
> **Aushrine, Lithuania**

What had happened? Breathlessly, she explained, "God has answered my prayers! I had a phone call; the husband of my daughter is in prison. Today he has been told his prison sentence has been shortened by nine months, and he is being freed!" She raised her arms to Heaven proclaiming in Russian, "Спасибо тебе, Иисус!" (Thank You, Jesus!). Truly, God's ways are not our ways. He heals and blesses as He wills.

TESTIMONIES FOR FUTURE GENERATIONS

During Jesus' earthly ministry, the miracles brought the people to hear the message of salvation. As T.B. Joshua often said,

> "A miracle is not an end in itself, but a means to an end - which is the salvation of your soul."

One of the Holy Spirit's instructions to him from the beginning of his ministry was to 'take the record'. His documentary My Story, for example, is thus supported by visual evidence from the earliest stages.

We have in the Bible a record of some of the miracles in the earthly ministry of Jesus Christ. We read how a man waiting at the Pool of Bethesda had been an invalid for 38 years; a woman who touched the hem of Jesus' garment had been bleeding for 12 years, having spent all her money on trying to find a cure. For these facts to have been recorded, someone must have interviewed the people who were healed.

"Jesus performed many other signs in the presence of his disciples, which are not recorded in this book. But these are written that you may believe that Jesus is the Messiah, the Son of God, and that by believing you may have life in his name." (John 20:30-31)

The purpose of the record in the Gospels is clear. It is to bring the reader to a position of saving faith in Jesus Christ.

T.B. Joshua's intense passion for seeing Jesus glorified and people saved drove the whole video ministry of The SCOAN and Emmanuel TV.

Early VHS Videos from The SCOAN

A video record was often taken before, during and after prayer. Visitors would receive copies of the resulting video testimonies to take home and use as the Holy Spirit directed them. 'Divine Miracles Part 5', the famous VHS tape including the man's healing from buttocks cancer, would go to many countries.

One of the early encouragements we received was to try to get the videos of miracles to a much wider audience. We showed our friends, but the bigger vision to achieve that, such as getting people together in a cinema or club to watch these mighty deliverances, seemed, wow, 'challenging'. How could it happen in the UK? Prophet T.B. Joshua, a man who looked beyond, was he seeing the future when Emmanuel TV would take YouTube by storm and people would watch the clips all over the world (cinema style) in their living rooms? Back then, in 2001 and 2002, online video sharing had not even been thought of.

As in other areas of life, there is God's part, and there is our part. God works the miracle, but there is a lot of our own work that has to go into recording the testimony of that miracle in a way that communicates clearly. That is why, usually, those coming for prayer to The SCOAN are interviewed during a time of registration and asked to provide an official medical report if their condition is a medical one. That time of interview is also an opportunity to counsel those seeking healing, and in some cases, to advise them to take more steps to build their faith in Jesus Christ first.

> *"After every single visit to The SCOAN, Jesus is changing our character, our habits and our mindset."*
> **Rytis, Lithuania**

Then during the actual prayer, the camera team is a crucial part of the ministry. After all, only a handful of people can see the prayer clearly in front of them; thousands more can see it on screens positioned around the church; potentially millions more can see it via live broadcasts and recorded clips. It therefore matters, for the glory of God, that the cameras have a clear view.

Tireless team members stay long after services have completed, interviewing those who have an immediate testimony or experience to share that will encourage others towards faith in Christ.

Divine Healing

"Divine healing is the supernatural power of God, bringing health to the human body."

The physical evidence of the supernatural causing changes to our body, which we call 'Divine Healing in the name of Jesus Christ', is not magic; it is not some abstract 'power'. We receive it by grace and maintain it by faith. Divine healing, deliverance and breakthrough are freely available through the cross of Jesus Christ.

As T.B. Joshua regularly teaches, healing in the Bible is a promise relating to Jesus' sacrifice on the cross,

"All the punishment Jesus Christ received before and during

His crucifixion was for our healing: spirit, soul and body."

"Christ paid for your perfect and complete healing when He died on the cross." (see 1 Peter 2:24)

"There is only one ground for claiming healing/ blessing/ salvation/ protection - by His wounds."

"You may not have experienced healing, but that does not mean He has not provided it; by His wounds, we are healed."

Many other men and women of faith through the years have also taught the principle of divine healing through the atonement. For example, A.B. Simpson (1843-1919), founder of the Christian and Missionary Alliance, wrote,

> The atonement of Jesus Christ covers our sicknesses and furnishes solid ground for claiming, in His name, divine healing through simple faith, and when we are walking in holy obedience, which, of course, is the indispensable element within which we can continue to receive any of the blessings of the Gospel.[12]

DON'T LIMIT GOD

Jesus has provided healing, but T.B. Joshua also teaches from the Bible that we should not limit God to certain answers to prayer.

"When you pray, you should not limit God to certain answers; let your prayer be of thanks, not just for what He has done alone but for what He is able to do, for we may not know how much we need Him. He is able to do more than we could ever dream."

We, as human beings, can be very demanding. We may sit quietly in the church, but these and other questions might be raging in our hearts:

- "It is all up to God; He is the one with the power; He can heal me if He wants to."

12 Simpson, A.B. (Aug 1890). *Divine Healing in the Atonement*, Christian and Missionary Alliance Weekly, pp. 122-124

- "I have saved and paid (or borrowed) a lot of money to come here; therefore, God must answer my prayer!"

- "My close relative is near to death; Jesus must touch her today."

- "I cannot stand my work situation any longer; the man of God must speak to me today."

- "I pray all night at the vigil; I do my fasting; I cry all day long; God, therefore, must hear me."

- "I have paid my tithes for many years, I am a good church member, and I help teach Sunday School. Why should all these sicknesses be afflicting me?'

- "I have spent all my money, visited all the well-known alternative therapists, Sangomas (herbalists, witchdoctors) in my country, but I am no better. Can this man of God help?"

- "I don't really believe in all this, but I have heard this pastor has some power; maybe he will help me."

The echoing theme running through all the encouragement given to those suffering is that Jesus never promised to keep believers away from difficult times or trials but to see us through. As T.B. Joshua would often explain,

"Whether Jesus heals me or not, He is my Healer; whether He blesses me or not, He is my Blessing Provider."

"To learn how to hear God after prayer is a much greater blessing than what you are looking for."

Again we see that Christianity is not a religion, a formula or a technique for success, but a personal relationship with God through Jesus Christ.

Evelin from Hungary is typical of many who have received divine healing through prayer at The SCOAN. The physical improvement is a great blessing, but the growth in relationship with God is an even greater one.

I lost my hearing in my right ear when I was a child. The reason was unknown, and in spite of different treatments and the removal of my tonsils, there was no improvement. Finally, the doctors told me that the nerves were damaged and there was no solution to my problem, which caused a lot of inconvenience in my everyday life. As an adult, I continued to receive the same diagnosis and apart from the use of a hearing aid, which was uncomfortable and awkward to use, there was no solution.

After more than thirty years of this deafness, just one touch from Heaven through the man of God, Prophet TB Joshua (in 2016) put an end to this condition. My ear was opened and my testimony went far and wide, reaching people in different nations and continents.

However, the greatest miracle was not my healing but the fact that I have had a share of the grace and anointing of a prophet of God, who gave me the greatest of all blessings: I have learned to follow God's process and timing and to pray according to His will by His Spirit. There are no words to express my gratitude; all I have is a life for Jesus.[13]

GOD AND MEDICINE

The fact that Jesus still heals today does not negate the medical profession's noble work in diagnosing and treating us when we are sick.

"If you can't trust God with medicine, you can't trust God without medicine."

T.B. Joshua proclaimed this message in a live Sunday service on Emmanuel TV. He repeated it, saying, "Write it down!"

It is not an 'either/or' situation - either you use medicine instead of trusting God, or you trust God instead of using medication. Rather it is about your relationship with God. If we do not believe that Jesus is with us through His Word, by His Spirit with our medical treatment, we may find it challenging to believe God for His promises in the Holy Bible for supernatural healing.

---

13   Private communication

From the many years of facilitating scores of international groups to visit The SCOAN, it has been apparent that there are many different opinions about healing and deliverance. These can range from those who believe the age of miracles died out when the Apostles passed away, that now God helps only through the wonders of modern medicine, to others who frame every symptom and sickness in spiritual terms, an attack that needs deliverance by prayer only.

We also encountered a school of thought that regards everything as being purchasable with money or demandable on our terms, especially when connected with health conditions that doctors could not help. However, just as the Bible's holiness is not for sale, healing is also not for sale or available because we shout loud enough. It revealed an assumption in the person that there must be somewhere this stored up 'power', and more pleading and demanding would force it out.

Different cultures would use different ways to describe their problems. Those coming from countries with more developed health services would talk about 'familial tendencies' to certain sicknesses, for example, heart problems and cancers running in their family. One would find that many such people would run to God as a last resort when all else appeared to have failed.

Those from cultures with different approaches to health, where people were as likely to consult the church or the local herbalist (witch doctor) as the medical doctor, would relate more to the term ancestral or family curse. Actually, whether referred to as familial tendencies or family curse, the effects in people's lives across the continents were often similar.

Some people would find that they would be more likely to have complications from their sickness, whilst others responded to treatment well. Some families were prone to dying at a younger age from illness or serious accidents, whilst others were spared. T.B. Joshua explains that when sickness becomes a curse, only Jesus can remove the curse.

Life is a battlefield. In one service, he was to say publicly, "Let me show you the face of cancer," and speaking a word of authority over a woman in the prayer line who was a cancer patient, the face instantly changed to an evil demonic countenance.

In some cases, a deliverance would lead to instant healing, while others would find their conditions would respond to treatment differently after prayer. We came to understand that there are no simple answers except to trust Jesus day by day through the storms and vicissitudes of life.

DOCTORS TREAT, GOD HEALS

From the earliest times of Christianity, Christians have been known for caring for the sick.

There are many examples of godly doctors and surgeons who have seen God as the one who inspires them to gain the specialist skills needed to perform complex surgical operations. There are also those godly believers whose research in medicine would lead to great discoveries to alleviate suffering. An example is Alexander Fleming, discoverer of antibiotics, who famously said, "The unprepared mind cannot see the outstretched hand of opportunity", and "Nature makes penicillin; I just found it."

God is indeed the God of nature, as T.B. Joshua has often said, and medications operate in the realm of nature. As a farmer exercises faith in nature, without a definite promise, when he plants a seed and expects it to grow without digging it up to check it, so believers in Christ should have faith in the God of nature, especially since they have so many promises recorded in the Bible.

T.B. Joshua has always maintained the greatest respect for the medical profession but has emphasised that God's servants and medical doctors should work together. Over the years, many people have asked for help for their conditions, where he has supported them to go for specialist medical treatment. In one such case, he explained,

When a patient is before me, I will ask God, 'What do you want me to do, Sir?' If God says, 'Take him to such a place' - I know my boundary. I must have a boundary because I am not God; it is only God who does not have a boundary. When it comes to issues like this, I am a servant. I can only do what I am given to do; I cannot do more than what is given to me.

So, this is an example of working together - God's servant and medical doctors. When someone is in the operation room, God's servant will be in an attitude of prayer throughout the operation, so that the doctor will not be the one that even does the operation, God will only use his hand to do the operation.[14]

"Man of God, please help me!" During a Sunday service, a young local Nigerian could not contain his emotion, "I was wounded doing my job for the bank, and the injuries I received are life-altering. I cannot pass urine normally, I have a catheter, and I am a young man..." His voice trailed off. T.B. Joshua understood.

Calling some medical doctors who were attending the service, he asked them to examine the young man called Gift privately and then took the situation to God for wisdom. Meanwhile, the young man with a beating heart began to have hope; someone cared about his condition. Christianity is practical.

Soon, the solution came; medical efforts to help him had failed in Nigeria, but a specialist hospital with surgeons trained to a higher level might be God's answer. And so it was to be. The ministry funded Mr Gift with two people accompanying him to fly to a pres-

Mr Gift Sharing his Testimony

tigious hospital in India with all expenses covered. This was a young man who had never previously entered a plane or owned an international passport. The complex

14   *If God's Servants And Medical Doctors Work Together,* TB Joshua Ministries Facebook Post, 14 Jul 2020

corrective surgery was performed successfully there.

Mr Gift returned, rejoicing to testify with a thankful heart that his body was now functioning, he could urinate normally, and the catheter was now a dim and distant memory.

Watching this, we were so grateful for the wisdom of God in instructing His servant to handle one situation one way and another a different way.

Sensitivity for the Vulnerable

One aspect of God's wisdom in T.B. Joshua concerned a caution about praying for those in the vulnerable category; this could include autistic children, those with mental impairments, and those with mental illness on serious long-term medication.

There is no suggestion that 'one size fits all' or that everyone needs deliverance ministry. We had travelled in places where vulnerable people were not treated with so much understanding, leading to potential pain and disappointment.

Early on, during a group visit from the UK, there was a salutary experience of what can happen when we come into the light in the 'arena of liberty', as The SCOAN eventually was to be called. A British businessman joined a visit to The SCOAN but omitted to mention his mental health problem and that he had been admitted more than once to a well known mental institution. Initially, on the prayer line, he greeted Prophet T.B. Joshua (as though meeting the Pope) by reverently kneeling before him and kissing his hand. However, he later appeared in the dining room wearing a loose white garment, looking mentally deranged with dishevelled hair, clutching a cross and making rude explicit comments to all. It was like a bad movie.

But T.B. Joshua, with wisdom from God, did not go into an 'exorcism' session. Instead, he made sure the man was well looked after and had someone with him so he would not do anything silly whilst 'not in his right mind'. He then spent time gently teaching the UK group, especially people who knew him, the difference between handling mental illness and demonic possession. The man responded to the love shown to him enough to be allowed on the plane home.

ANOINTED BIBLE TEACHING

The group visits to The SCOAN were also times of spiritual nourishment in studying the Word of God. We sat in the plastic chairs with our Bibles lovingly clasped on our knees, waiting for an all too brief teaching session.

"The Jesus I know," T.B. Joshua would tell us, "Is Jesus in the power of the Holy Spirit". He warned us not to read the Bible with offence and unforgiveness in our hearts. He took us on a journey to understand that,

> "The book of Acts is not history but the pattern of how the church should be."

One could begin to understand 'as through a glass darkly' how the 'Holy' part of the Holy Bible is a treasure chest of rich jewels. It is not the Bible of history and architecture and ancient civilisations stretching back to the very dawn of time, but the Bible of holiness, repentance, conviction, comfort and succour, the Bread of life, Water to the thirsty and a Roadmap to the lost.

It appeared that all who wanted to seek first the kingdom of God and His righteousness devoured the Bible teaching by T.B. Joshua, appreciating its simplicity and depth. On the other hand, those

'Mouthpiece of God' Sermon Notes from 2003

more interested in receiving an impartation of power appeared less aware of its importance. The Bible teaching came packaged with bite-sized quotes, which were referred to as 'quotable quotes'. These were like modern-day proverbs, for example,

> "True humility means total dependence on God for everything."

> "With your words, you constantly paint a public picture of your inner self."

Many of these quotes came as a result of T.B. Joshua meditating continually on the Bible. They were taken very seriously by the church members and always appeared in the church sermon notes, which were given to the visitors and bought weekly and treasured by the church members.

The teaching was so instructive that some groups of visitors would watch the Bible teaching videos in the dining room and take notes; then, we would all sit together and discuss them. Each would be saying, "What did you write down? Let me look so I can expand my notes."

Later as the number of international visitors grew, there would be regular Bible Teaching slots with question and answer sessions at the end of each teaching. The visitors thoroughly enjoyed these.

T.B. Joshua would explain that our relationship with God could be

A More Recent SCOAN Sermon Note

'deep', 'deeper' or 'deepest'. Very soon, the desire created by the Bible teaching to have 'more of God' was more important than comparing the miracles or 'raw confessions'. After a visit to The SCOAN, one was more aware of sin, more humble, more forgiving, less inclined to gossip, one loved the Bible more and wanted to read it more. The presence of God in His Holy Word was real. As ever, the issue was to maintain it.

To the Nations

The first set of large international Gospel events (using various titles depending on the host country's sensitivities) took place between 2005 and 2007, showing that this work of God could cross national and cultural boundaries and remain essentially the same. This may in no small measure be because T.B.Joshua himself remained the same, maintaining the same devotion to prayer and the same commitment to obey God rather than please people, whether in Lagos or abroad.

Except for an earlier event in Ghana, we have had the privilege of being present and often part of the advance team for all the large International Gospel Events (crusades) with T.B. Joshua.

BOTSWANA FOR CHRIST

With joy in our hearts, we travelled to the vast country of Botswana in Southern Africa, with its relatively small population, to join the team helping prepare for T.B. Joshua's coming to the capital, Gabarone. We flew to Johannesburg, drove from South Africa to the border, and met with the Gabarone heat. Staying with a local family with no air

Fiona in Botswana, March 2005

conditioning, just a simple fan, was good practice for our future Emmanuel TV trips to Pakistan. There, the electricity supply was one hour on and one hour off, and there was definitely no air conditioning. A last-minute team request to source some national flags saw us finding a sports fan shop to get the necessary quantity at short notice.

T.B. Joshua's Arrival in Botswana

We were there with many others for T.B. Joshua's arrival in Botswana on 7 March 2005.

"I am so excited," one lady commented to her neighbour, "T.B. Joshua is coming to our country. You know I visited The SCOAN last year, and truly, my life has been different since."

"Where did you get that Botswana national flag?"

"Go and ask those British people; they are giving them out."

"Wait, there is the car! Is that him?"

"He is getting out! He is dressed so simply!"

"He is speaking to us!"

"It is time to speak with our mouth what we believe in our heart."

"I am here for what I was born for, what I am living for, and what I will die for - to tell people about Jesus the Saviour, Healer and Deliverer."

There was no small talk, no wasted words, just an expression of what was in his heart.

On the first night of the crusade in the national football stadium, T.B. Joshua spoke to a young man who had to use crutches to walk following a car accident,

"You should be ready to look beyond healing. Seek salvation. The salvation of your soul is what I am here for."

Showing his X-rays of the screws put into his bones and complaining of the pain, the young man called Godfrey cried out in response,

"I want Jesus to heal me completely."

"Healing is not an end in itself; it is a means to an end. You should be ready to follow Jesus. When you are healed, find a living church. Anyone can receive blessing, but not everyone can maintain it."

"I am ready to follow Jesus after my healing."

"Do not go where Jesus would not be welcomed."

Then Mr Godfrey received prayer and miraculous healing, returning the next day to give public testimony and demonstrate that he no longer needed his crutches.

Prophet T.B. Joshua walked among the crowds on that football pitch for hours, praying for many like Mr Godfrey and giving accurate personal prophecies to many others.

Mr Godfrey Receives Healing in Botswana

Then, in the early hours of the morning, he prayed for rain. Botswana was in a severe drought, adversely affecting its farming industry, integral to the nation's infrastructure. As he offered the prayer while standing on the pitch in that stadium, we marvelled as some rain instantly began falling – a divine sign of the changes in the nation's climate that quickly followed.

KOREA FOR CHRIST

Over the next few years, T.B. Joshua would visit several Asian countries for the Gospel.

A series of South Korean visitors had made the long journey to The

SCOAN because they had heard of all God was doing. An Invitation was forthcoming and was to herald the start of three significant events in South Korea. The first venue was the Anyang Sports Complex near Seoul.

It was May 2005, and Prophet T.B. Joshua was praying for individuals for healing and deliverance. One example of the many miracles was for a young lady who explained that she had broken her leg due to an accident and now couldn't walk without crutches. She explained tearfully, "I want to run!" Following the prayer, for all to see, she then began to run freely.

A Young Lady Receives Healing in Korea, 2005

Seeing T.B. Joshua praying for a girl with walking problems, we noted she reverently held his hand and kissed it. This kind of encounter was to be repeated over the years; there would be children declaring "I love you" to the man of God completely unprompted.

Word had got around that a man with an anointed healing ministry was in town, and large numbers of people crowded the sports complex looking for healing. They needed to hear the message! The crusade was arranged over four days and, led by the Holy Spirit, Prophet T.B. Joshua preached messages that addressed some critical issues for receiving divine healing.

The Korea for Christ Crusade in 2005

In the first message, *Your Role Part 1*, he made clear that receiving healing or redemption is not all up to God; we also have a role to play, which is to believe. In part 2 of this message, he emphasised, "I am not the healer, I have no power of my own. I am not God; I am His servant. I can only go where God wants me to go."

The third message was about sin, Your Actual Enemy. "Your enemy satan cannot rule, control or command you without sin. So, therefore, sin is your actual enemy." The final message was an encouragement that God is Good all the Time. Teaching from the life of Job, he encouraged the crowd, "Whether you are healed or not, whether Prophet T.B. Joshua attends to you or not, stay true to Jesus, because healing is for the salvation of your soul."

Following the crusade, a Pastors' Conference was held at a Prayer Mountain retreat centre outside the city. When T.B. Joshua prayed for the pastors for impartation, it was like a wild revival meeting, with pastors falling and overcome with joy without even being touched. Even the SCOAN cameramen did not escape the

The 2005 Pastors Conference in Korea with T.B. Joshua

anointing, struggling to remain standing while being 'zapped' by the Holy Spirit. The Holy Spirit was at work; as ever, the issue for everyone affected was to maintain the presence of God rather than subsequently losing it.

AUSTRALIA FOR CHRIST

A Member of Parliament Welcomes Visitors to the Australia for Christ Crusade with T.B. Joshua in 2006

The Australia for Christ crusade was an outdoor event held at the

Blacktown International Sportspark in Sydney on 24th and 25th March 2006. The local Mayor and a Member of Parliament gave the official welcomes. The Christian minister introducing T.B. Joshua was the respected elderly evangelist Bill Subritzky from New Zealand. He had visited The Synagogue, Church Of All Nations with a group of Pastors. On his return, he had been instrumental in testifying to what God was doing through T.B. Joshua by promoting the miracle videos. He was well aware of the controversies and persecution surrounding the ministry. On the opening night, he attested how God was using T.B. Joshua mightily, ending his introduction with the words, "So Praise God for this ministry!"

T.B. Joshua and Bill Subritzky During the Altar Call

Apart from the remarkable cases of healing, deliverance and prophecy, another notable feature of the main event was the Altar Call, a response to the message of salvation, which was conducted jointly by Bill Subritzky and T.B. Joshua.

For one particular man, his life began to change when Prophet T.B. Joshua walked straight to him on the sports field and began to prophesy. He told him that he saw he was a drug addict and that his son would come back into his life. He held onto that prophecy until it finally came to pass. In 2016, he received a knock on his door, and the son he hadn't known for 21 years was standing in front of him. An incredible reunion followed, which led to his son starting to live in his house. In 2017, he visited The SCOAN to confirm the prophecy and testify how it had changed his life.

After the main outdoor event, there were two other significant meetings. The first was a Pastors' Conference held at Bowman Hall, Blacktown, which was packed out; many wanted to hear from him. The conference started with some testimonies from the crusade, including one lady who had risen from her wheelchair and now appeared beautifully dressed wearing high heeled shoes. She joyfully testified to her healing from osteoporosis and rheumatoid arthritis.

T.B. Joshua preached a sermon titled 'This Kind' (taken from Mark 9:29), which explained that there are different levels of believing and hence different levels of fulfilment of the promise that "all things are possible to him who believes" (Mark 9:23). He emphasised that what restricts our capacity to believe is on the inside, not the outside; therefore, we need to reset our belief. How? By following the instructions in the book of Joshua 1:8, to keep the Word of God on our lips, meditate on it day and night, and then do what it says.

Following the sermon and a time of prayer for sanctification, he began to prophesy. The first prophecy was for a woman with a 'spirit of snake'. Immediately, a young white lady stepped forward and, with a tremulous voice, explained in her distinctive Australian accent that she had joined a cult as a teenager where they ate raw dead snakes in order for the spirit of the snake to enter. Prayer for deliverance and a joyful testimony of freedom followed.

The second additional meeting was for businessmen. The preaching by T.B. Joshua did not pull any punches and was in many ways a prophetic warning for the Western world. He reminded everyone that death was coming, and they didn't know when, so they should be ready. They should give God the best of their time, not rushing to church and putting time limits on God.

Throughout history, there have been accounts of servants of God in which simply being near them, or objects which they have recently handled, elicits some surprising reactions. After the crusade in Australia, T.B. Joshua accompanied the team to eat in a restaurant in Sydney. After he had briefly eaten and left the restaurant, some of the team who remained witnessed this unusual scene. The waitress who came to clear the table picked up the plate he had been eating from; instantly, she dropped it, started shaking and behaving abnormally, apparently manifesting an evil spirit. Recovering herself, she asked, "Who is that man?"

National Healing Campaign, Singapore

Because of local rules reflecting Singapore's religious diversity, the 'crusade' title had to be more 'neutral', so the local organisers chose National Healing Campaign. It was a substantial campaign, with no fewer than seven public meetings over the period from 26 November to 3 December 2006. These were an

An Advert on the Singapore Metro for the National Healing Campaign

opening service at one of the host churches, two 'crusade' nights in the national indoor stadium, a pastors and leaders' meeting, a businessman's dinner, a 'marketplace' lunch and a youth rally. Following these, there was a memorable visit by T.B. Joshua to the prison, where dressed in prison uniform, he shared with the prisoners and prayed for them.

On the second night at the indoor stadium, T.B. Joshua did not come to the service when the organising pastors expected him. They looked concerned and started to fill the time by getting different local pastors on stage to talk about their work. We looked at each other and at our watches many times and wondered what was happening. Was this tardiness related in any way to the well known perceived cultural tendency of 'African time'? But on the other side of this drama,

Prophet T.B. Joshua was about to leave his accommodation 'in good time', when, with his hand on the door to leave, the Holy Spirit spoke to his heart to wait.

When he finally arrived, he gave a concise and powerful evangelistic message explaining that the only permanent solution

A Time of Worship During the National Healing Campaign with T.B. Joshua

to our problems was in the forgiveness of sins through faith in Christ. Then, he dispensed with the 'normal' programme and went straight into a time of 'mass prayer', initially for deliverance from evil spirits and then for healing. We wrote about this time when we saw 'the Gospels in action' at the beginning of this book. As the whole stadium repeated the name of Jesus in unison, the author-ity and power of God were awe-in-spiring. It was something we hadn't witnessed before, even in the services at The SCOAN in Lagos. As referred to earlier, we even saw the anointing of God bring healing and deliverance to many when we played the video of this mass prayer years later to crowds in Pakistan and elsewhere.

Mass Prayer in Singapore

What would have happened if T.B. Joshua had not heeded the inti-mation of the Holy Spirit and had arrived 'on time'? Who knows? But one thing is sure, if he hadn't had the 'free spirit' and 'peace of heart' that comes from obeying only God, there is no way we could have witnessed those events, nor that those multitudes could have received their deliverance and healing in God's appointed way and at God's appointed time.

This was not the only 'test of faith' that was evident during the Singa-pore campaign. There were also several cases where those seeking healing from significant problems had to wait and show their will-ingness to come more than once. On one occasion following the Marketplace Lunch, where people were not necessarily expecting there to be a prayer line, T.B. Joshua explained this clearly. He had finished the message on "The Purpose of Blessing" and started to pray for those seeking healing. Here is what we noted down from what he said,

> For many of us, it is not the laying on of hands that we need, but it is instruction on what to do. Obey the word, and your

case will be settled.

> If healing is not for you now, I will not pray for you. I do not practice prayer. Your healing may be tomorrow, and it may be someone else praying for you. It's not everyone here that I'm sent to.

Referring to a lady who was present there in a wheelchair, he said,

> Yesterday, I was with her for some time, and she could not walk. The Spirit of God said, 'Invite her tomorrow'.

We then watched as T.B. Joshua prayed for her, and she instantly stood from the wheelchair and walked. He went on to say,

> I invited three, but I only see this one here. One man, his miracle is now, but he is not here. When Elisha said, 'Go to the Jordan seven times', he did not say once. When Jesus said, 'Go and wash in the pool', it was not because He did not have the power; it was to test the man's faith. Whatever problem you have, you should expect tests of faith.

This was typical of so many' impromptu sermons' we have heard from him during ministry, another example of 'practical Christianity'.

INDONESIA

T.B. Joshua in Jakarta, 2007

The Indonesia Crusade with Prophet T.B. Joshua took place in Jakarta and Surabaya at the end of September 2007.

It was clear that there had been much debate and controversy about the coming of T.B. Joshua to Indonesia. On the first night, in Jakarta in the Indoor Stadium, he addressed the controversy directly and preached about Nicodemus from John 3:1-12,

> Many people develop hatred or love about a particular person because of what they hear, what they read or what they see.

Nicodemus never did this. He was not the kind of person that would be swayed by what people said. Being a man of principle, he decided to come to Jesus to confirm. He did not sit somewhere hearing this or that and come to a hasty conclusion.

Later during that first meeting, there was one particularly dramatic deliverance as T.B. Joshua moved along the prayer line to pray for hundreds of people. One man, appearing quite normal on the outside, instantly fell backwards and started to shake as T.B. Joshua touched him. He then appeared to go into some form of trance, and from his mouth came the words, not in his own language but in English, "I am Beelzebub, a servant of Lucifer." At one stage, he pointed his finger at the man of God, saying, "I know you. I am angry at you." Following some boastful words spoken by the demon inside the man, wanting to fight God's servant, T.B. Joshua asked a young boy standing nearby to pray for the man, who fell back, demonstrating that the power was not his but belongs to Jesus. The man returned with his whole family for the subsequent Leaders' event and publicly shared his testimony in his own language, thanking Jesus for His love in remembering him and setting him free.

Following the crusade, T.B. Joshua visited the House of Love, a charity home established to take care of homeless and rejected people in Surabaya. Here he shared the love of Christ and donated US $10,000 to the charity's founders in support of their work.

FIRE IN THE CONSOLE

After the crusade in Indonesia, back in The SCOAN, the crackling of fire was to be heard one night. Evangelists sleeping after a busy service day received a call, "Wake up, the console with all the equipment so vital for Emmanuel TV is on fire! We trust it will not spread to the roof of the church. Quick, run, every moment is valuable." The visitors staying in the church were moved to a safe place, and the tension was rising.

One evangelist was to relate many years later in a Sunday sermon that, troubled in heart, he began helping bring buckets of water only to hear someone behind him appearing unperturbed. Affronted, he turned around and found himself looking right into the calm eyes of T.B. Joshua, who asked him, "How are you?"

T.B. Joshua did not fluctuate with the vicissitudes of life. He exemplified that the "peace which passes understanding" spoken of in the Bible is not related to the absence of trouble but rather to an assurance that God will see us through.

Indeed, as the night wore on, the church roof escaped damage, no one was hurt, and although Emmanuel TV was to go off air for three months, the equipment was eventually replaced and a new, better console built.

Shortly after the incident, T.B. Joshua publicly reflected,

"When the recent fire incident occurred in The Synagogue, as a man of persevering faith, I knew that satan was only trying to provoke me into rebelling against my Heavenly Father. Little did he know that God uses the affliction of the saints to promote their fruitfulness (Genesis 41:52; Jeremiah 17:7-8)."

INTERNATIONAL EVENTS RESUME

After a gap of years, which saw the development of the large SCOAN Sunday services with a strong international flavour and the continued growth of Emmanuel TV, it was time! The year was 2014, and T.B. Joshua heard the 'yes' from God to travel again. Now the technical questions would begin. After all the training and experience in live recording and transmission of the Sunday services, could the team (with appropriate local technical assistance) now manage live broadcasting from International Events worldwide, especially the forthcoming outdoor stadium events?

It was early 2014; arriving at The SCOAN late at night, having helped with some camera equipment orders, there came a knock on the door of the room. Rubbing our eyes, we saw an evangelist smiling,

"Baba, Mama, welcome! (older parents are always known as Baba and Mama in African culture) T.B. Joshua wants you to meet some pastors who are about to travel."

Quickly making ourselves ready, we greeted the two pastors from Colombia, little realising that within months the long gap between the Indonesia event in 2007 and the future was coming to an end, and the huge Cali, Colombia event was approaching.

Then a few days later, there was another call. "Mama, Baba, come upstairs." We sat down and were told, "Look, there is a provisional date planned for the man of God to be in South Korea for a Pastor's conference." The evangelist held a calendar, and we saw the date circled and gasped. It was only one week away.

God's ways are mysterious. We thought we had gone to Lagos, at our own suggestion, just to guarantee safe delivery of some cameras, but God had other ideas. That night we set off to fly to Korea as part of an advance team.

After two overnight flights, the team arrived in Korea and got straight to work - the proposed Pastors Conference itself was now only six days away! Unrolling our traditional Korean sleeping mats in a friendly church's guest area, we thanked God for the opportunity to be part of this venture of faith. Whilst the other team members were researching potential places for prayer for T.B. Joshua (Prayer Mountains), we were on the team working with our hosts to find somewhere for the team to stay. Somewhat unsure of the various choices offered and knowing the whole team needed to be together, we reported the challenge to T.B. Joshua. The instruction then came back that the team would need to focus entirely on the job, including live broadcasting on Emmanuel TV, so we should look for suitable hotel accommodation. The ministry would pay; it would not be any burden for the hosts.

That quick exchange set the tone for the financing for the next five years of crusades when the ministry would pay most of the costs associated with a stadium event and all the team's travel and hotel costs. Most importantly, the ministry would not collect any offering. The organisers would collect an offering for their part of the expenses (before the SCOAN team came on stage), but T.B. Joshua would have no involvement in people's money when coming for healing.

거울

"The Mirror" Printed in Korean

Also, from that time onwards, no books or DVDs were sold at the stadium events; they were all given away. The production and printing in different languages of T.B. Joshua's study book on heroes of faith in the Bible, *The Mirror*, became a regular part of crusade preparation. The same was true of his booklet on receiving and maintaining healing from God, *The Step Between You And The Cure.*

T.B. Joshua very rarely wrote a book. He was himself a living letter as 2 Corinthians 3: 2 says,

"You yourselves are our letter, written on our hearts, known and read by everyone."

The only other books published by The SCOAN have been *Daily Time With God*, a collection of quotes, and *What The Future Holds (I and II)*, which are journals of some of the international prophecies given by Prophet T.B. Joshua over the years.

LIVE TRANSMISSION ON EMMANUEL TV

One of the practical reasons that the 2014 Korea Pastors' Conference had been possible to finalise at such short notice was that it was held in a well-equipped church building, with much of the technical infrastructure already in place. For example, the church was already experienced with live internet streaming, and so the infrastructure for this was already set up.

Gary takes up the story,

Shortly before the event, the message came from T.B. Joshua that the conference should be broadcast live on Emmanuel TV. In a pre-service test, the Emmanuel TV transmission centre (at that time in South Africa) simply logged in to the church's internet stream, and everything worked well. However, shortly after the conference started, the network crashed. We discovered that the existing arrangements had a somewhat limited capacity, which couldn't cope with the extra numbers trying to join the church internet stream locally to view the conference.

We needed an immediate solution. The streaming was provided via a third party company that was not responding. I managed to connect my laptop to the public internet and set up a new stream to connect directly with

the Emmanuel TV transmission centre, but the cables and converters needed to get the live video into the laptop were not available. Then I remembered I could connect my domestic video camera to my laptop, so we strapped it to a tripod with sticky tape and pointed it at the 'programme monitor' in the control room.

A Successful 'Heath Robinson' Solution to a Live Transmission Problem

Holding their breath, back in South Africa, the Emmanuel TV technical team waited! Would the homespun solution work? Yes, it did. Finally, the team could report that the first international event outside Nigeria for seven years with T.B. Joshua was now broadcasting live both on African satellite channels and on the internet. If the video quality left a bit to be desired, the real business of the event - the anointed prayer and teaching - was reaching the international audience.

For future events, it was to become an essential part of the technical planning, and live transmission with full high definition quality became the norm.

THE DANGERS OF MONEY

The 2014 Pastors Conference with T.B. Joshua in South Korea

While entrance to all the international events has been free of charge, at the South Korea Pastors Conference, entry was free, but the team discovered that "partner donors" who supported the organisers to a certain level were offered a seat in a section closer to the front, where Prophet T.B. Joshua was expected to pray for people. But the Holy Spirit does as He wills, and when the time came for individual prayer, the ministry started with people seated on the balcony!

At that Pastors' Conference, T.B. Joshua spoke openly and frankly on the issue of money and explained why he had stopped travelling internationally for a period. (It was certainly not a lack of invitations.)

> Healing, deliverance, prophecy and all of God's blessings are hindered by money. It is not possible to heal people and collect money. When it is time to heal, it is time to give what God has given us.

> When it is time for revival or crusade, it is time to hear the will of God. If it is the will of God for revival, what to use, money to spend, the Lord will provide it in a big way - not from the sick ones or people coming, but God will provide it in a wonderful way. I asked God that before I begin to move for revival, I want Him to raise my standard financially.[15]

Then he expanded on this during a sermon at the church in Lagos in 2017:

> All these crusades you see me doing around the world, such as in Singapore, Indonesia, Mexico, Peru etc. – I pay most of

---

15   Pastors Conference with T.B. Joshua, Shingil Church, Seoul, 2-3 April 2014

the money. We don't control the Holy Spirit! When I am there, I want to be free. I want to sleep at the time the Spirit wants me to sleep. I want to pray for who the Holy Spirit wants me to pray for.

If you pay for the stadium for me, you will collect money from big businessmen that are sick, and they will be the ones you arrange in front, telling me, "Pray for this one, Man of God, he is the one who paid seventy per cent of the money". God cannot support such an arrangement. You are telling me to come out at 8 am when the Spirit of God said I can come out at 10 am. So, I pay for the stadium.

My joy is to see people healed; my joy is to see people delivered; my joy is to see people blessed. That is my money. Each person that is delivered is more than $20,000 to me! That is the money God gives me, the joy to sleep in peace.[16]

Over the years, we have seen this principle clearly in operation and experienced its blessings, which far outweigh any challenges.

CALI, COLOMBIA

We come now to July 2014, and the Cruzada de Milagros con T.B. Joshua in Cali, Colombia. We spent two months in Colombia in the run-up to this event, which was to be on a new scale for all of us. It was to see the Olympic Football Stadium in the city filled to its 40,000-plus capacity over both nights.

The Miracle Crusade with T.B. Joshua in the Olympic Stadium, Cali, Colombia

Nearly 20 years previously, praying Christians had filled the same stadium, following the martyrdom of a prominent pastor in the city, which had led to a revival of faith. But as the local pastors explained, the revival fires had since receded with time, and the event was warmly anticipated. The believers were planning to bring those outside the church who needed to hear the Gospel preached with power.

During the sermon on the second night of the crusade, Prophet T.B. Joshua specifically addressed the state of the church,

> For anyone to talk, to preach, to teach about the Word and the Spirit in separation, it is biblically incorrect. We cannot continue like this because we are making Jesus Christ unpopular.
>
> The future of the church depends on our learning from each other. I need you; you need me. I need your theology; you need my power. I need your power; you need my theology.
>
> Because there is no union between the Word and the Spirit, this church is known for preaching and teaching the Word of God, while the other church is known for miracles, signs and wonders. This is not how it should be.
>
> I pray every day to see when we will no longer fight, envy and be jealous of one another.[17]

We saw that many churches did join hands in supporting the crusade. The President of the Confederación Evangelica De Colombia (Cedecol), representing most of the evangelical churches in Colombia, attended and spoke very positively of the Word of God and miracles coming together in the ministry of Prophet T.B. Joshua.

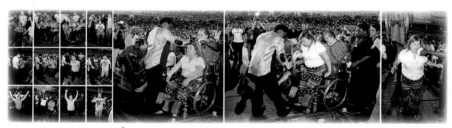

Healing on The Prayer Line in Cali, Colombia

---

17   *The Price of Faith Part 2*, Miracle Crusade with TB Joshua, Cali, Colombia, 12 Jul 2014

There were scores of healings and hundreds of deliverances, and the name of Jesus was lifted high. The late Evangelist C.S. Upthegrove, who had worked with many of the USA's prominent healing evangelists in the 1950s, attended the crusade, aged in his mid-80s. He expressed himself thrilled at having seen God work again so powerfully in healing and miracles.

The Mass Prayer in Cali, Colombia

One of the many remarkable healings of the crusade took place following the mass prayer, while the crowd sang, *There is power in the name of Jesus*. As the power of God swept across the stadium, the feet of a young girl, crooked since birth, miraculously straightened. As her braces were removed, she began to jump and run, the infectious joy lighting her face conveying a message beyond the expression of words.

Among the additional events in Cali, a city that knew what it was like to experience violence, was a substantial charity outreach. Several hundred families were invited, with transportation provided, for hot food and entertainment, a professional medical check-up for the children, and to receive a large bag of groceries.

T.B. Joshua at the Charity Event in Cali, Colombia

The Cali Metropolitan Police also hosted an event where they presented T.B. Joshua with an Honorary Award and his own Police Cap. He gave a generous US $100,000 gift to the social fund for those orphaned, widowed or

The Police Meeting with T.B. Joshua in Cali, Colombia

injured in the course of duty and shared a message of his appreciation of the police force's work, "You prevent crime in the society in the natural. We prevent crime in the spirit. We are doing the same job. I salute you."

THE MEXICO CRUSADE

The miracle crusade with Prophet T.B. Joshua in Mexico City in July 2015 was itself a phenomenon. How was it that the largest football stadium in Latin America was filled for a free Christian event for the first time in its history? The local organisers' hard work, travelling the length and breadth of Mexico, envisioning and encouraging different churches played a significant role, as did the production and distribution of thousands of free DVDs. However, in the end, this was a sovereign work of God.

Before the event, the team, including the camera crew, sat high up in

Miracle Crusade with Prophet T.B. Joshua in Mexico, 2015

the topmost seats for a planning meeting; we could not help feeling some 'prickles' of anxiety. It was so high, what would happen during the Mass Prayer when people reacted? 'God is with us', we encouraged ourselves, 'He will protect', and so it was to be.

The iconic world-famous 100,000-seat Aztec stadium was pretty well full on the second night of the crusade. The rain was heavy on the first night but, completely unperturbed, T.B. Joshua continued praying for hours, and the miracles happened. Fiona and other Emmanuel TV partners were out at the gates giving away the free DVDs of the Colombia Crusade as eventually, the rain slowed and the crowds began to leave. Night two was spared the downpour and was unforgettable. The work of God increased, and the testimonies were almost countless.

Prayer in the Rain on the First Night

The crowd was also treated to a surprise, with some faith-building musical contributions from well-known Gospel artists from the USA - CeCe Winans, Alvin Slaughter and Vashawn Mitchell.

An aptitude for physical work was a requirement, as the evangelists and team of helpers had to move everything from the stadium and store the remaining resources in the hotel at the end of the crusade. We all remembered running around directing and getting trucks into the right place to pick up the resources. In the end, the team would not enter their rooms until after 4 am, knowing that *'The joy of the Lord is our strength'* (Nehemiah 8:10).

Mass Prayer in Mexico

The crusade and the large Pastors Conference that followed it had a tremendous impact. A team from The SCOAN stayed on for several weeks to record follow-up testimonies and to edit the mass of video footage. We personally even moved to live in Mexico for over a year to help with follow-up, especially charity work. T.B. Joshua helped set up a local 'Civil Association' to support this.

T.B. Joshua himself could have spent more time in Mexico, but as he explained in a message he gave in the church in Lagos in 2017, his call from God was to return to Africa,

> I will go for revivals, and at the revivals, you will always see the stadium full. The country, ministers - all of them gather. But I am not carried away by that; after the crusade - back home. Back to Africa, where I am being persecuted, where they want me to be killed, destroyed. I live where I am not celebrated; I left the place where I am celebrated.
>
> When you are in the midst of battle, you are building yourself; it's good. Where you are not celebrated, where you are being persecuted, is the best place for you to live. It will build you. Gold cannot be gold without passing through the furnace. Human character, too, needs to pass through the furnace.[18]

CRUSADE WITH T.B. JOSHUA IN PERU

Following a dynamic second crusade in South Korea, held in the Gocheok Sky Dome in Seoul on 22 and 23 July 2016, T.B. Joshua returned to Latin America for another miracle crusade. It was to be in the largest football stadium in South America, the Monumental Stadium in Lima, Peru, in September 2016.

Crusade at the Monumental Stadium, Lima, Peru

The most memorable feature for us was the knife-edge timing. There was an administrative hold up with the visas for the Emmanuel TV team coming from Lagos. From a logistical planning point of view, decisions to confirm the crusade were all left to the latest possible time. But then those 'final' deadlines passed without final resolution

---

18   *Don't Destroy Your Relationships Beyond Repair,* Sermon by T.B. Joshua, SCOAN Sunday Service, 30 Apr 2017

of the visa delays, and it was only God who could enable the crusade to go ahead. The event was confirmed only two weeks before the planned date, and the full planning and organisational team from The SCOAN arrived just eleven days before the first night. From a natural point of view, there simply wasn't enough time to put together the necessary 'pieces of the jigsaw' to make it happen, but God had said, 'Go' to His servant, and that was all that mattered.

This forcefully reminded us that there are real benefits in having jobs that are 'impossible'. We should do the best we can, but in the end, it has to be God, and only He can take the glory.

The crusade itself showed no signs of these tensions; God was in control. From the legal permissions obtained in record-breaking time to the 300 ham and cheese baguettes that our team of Emmanuel TV partners had to arrange with virtually no notice (for the Police patrols working with the crowds) to the miracles of healing and deliverance - we needed God for everything.

A memorable moment was when Prophet T.B. Joshua stopped praying for people and sat down because there was a risk the crowd would surge forward. He said he wasn't moving until the people returned to their seats, which they duly did.

T.B. Joshua Waits for the Crowd to Settle

CRUSADES IN PARAGUAY AND DOMINICAN REPUBLIC

Paraguay is a smaller South American country, and its national stadium hosted the Crusade with T.B. Joshua in August 2017. Paraguay's National Parliament bestowed on him the nation's highest honour to recognise his Gospel and Humanitarian work. There were also remarkable testimonies from the crusade, including a significant deliverance for someone who wasn't even present but whose sister took a photograph of him for prayer.

For the 'backroom team', one challenge was that there was no suitable supplier in the whole of Paraguay for the temporary protective flooring needed to cover the football pitch for such events. The flooring was eventually sourced from an adjacent country, but it arrived late due to customs and logistical issues.

Laying the Temporary Pitch Covering for the Crusade in Paraguay

The whole SCOAN team - evangelists, cameramen, protocol, etc., and Emmanuel TV Partners who had offered to help - personally placed and then later removed the thousands of pieces of floor covering on the pitch. The stadium pitch had people crawling on their knees, sticking down the flooring with domestic sticking tape, a surreal experience.

Between the first and second days of the crusade, severe storms threatened the whole technical installation, and the stage banner ripped under the strong winds. T.B. Joshua declared to the entire stadium that "Rain is a servant of God, and we too are servants of God; rain cannot hinder us". He explained how he had in prayer "negotiated with the rain", requesting it to abate for the hours of the event so the technical equipment would be safe and the second day could proceed.

The rain did pause until after the mass prayer, but then it came in torrents, and it was cold. Looking after the people with testimonies who arrived at the interview rooms shivering with thin cotton T-shirts, we gave them warm hugs as well as food and shelter.

The Dominican Republic Crusade with T.B. Joshua in 2017

Just three short months later, in November 2017, was the Dominican Republic Crusade held in the capital Santo Domingo's Olympic Stadium.

What a beautiful event! What unity amongst the churches. As part of the technical team, we arrived early and were able to see this in action. The choirs practising sounded heavenly, and such willingness pervaded everywhere. A warm team spirit across cultures, colours and backgrounds was evident in the local believers. If there was a concern, it was whether all the people who wanted to come would fit in the 40,000 capacity stadium. Indeed many had to listen from the park outside.

T.B. Joshua was again presented with a high National Honour, and the country's President personally received him.

It was a colourful event as the dancers glorified Jesus, the warm Caribbean wind caressed our cheeks, and with the sun going down, the heat of the day evaporating, the real business of the day began.

T.B. Joshua with President Medina of the Dominican Republic

For the first night's message, T.B. Joshua gave a fundamental but straightforward sermon on the essence of Christianity: "Seek First the Kingdom". The proof text from Romans 5:1-8 reminded Christians about justification through faith based on Jesus' sacrificial death on the cross. The man of God also urged the audience to amass only spiritual treasures and to be committed to others' welfare and well-being.

There were public testimonies from previous crusades, prayer and deliverance and the blessing at the end, the mass prayer. Stadium mass prayer with T.B. Joshua is a powerful experience tempered with the fear of God. It is not an emotional time. It is a time when, as a helper, one genuinely does not know what will happen. Who will manifest? Who will vomit, who will drop their crutches or their walkers and stand up from their wheelchairs? As in every event, the helpers and team are ready for action, with practical footwear and identifying T-shirts.

"Camera, come quickly!" What is happening? Blood oozes from the head of a young woman. She has not fallen over; it is a supernatural event. She had suffered from a strange fungal infection on her scalp, which was both painful and shameful. She did not even receive a physical touch of prayer at The Dominican Republic Crusade With Prophet T.B. Joshua but the Holy Spirit Himself touched her during the time of Mass Prayer in a memorable manner. The infection vanished after her head started to bleed during the prayer, as she later testified alongside her aunt.

The UK and Israel

The Emmanuel TV UK Revival in Sheffield, 2019

There were events for several thousand people each in the UK, France and Argentina in 2018, all broadcast live, where Evangelists sent by T.B. Joshua offered prayer with Anointed Water in the mighty name of Jesus Christ. There were plentiful healings and deliverances following.

Then in 2019, the Holy Spirit directed towards two international events in June. The Emmanuel TV UK Revival was held in the Sheffield Arena, a large indoor stadium, with ministry by three of the current 'prophets in training'.

People came from far and wide to experience the anointing, and many had to be turned away as the stadium with over 10,000 seats was full.

T.B. Joshua remained in Lagos at the Prayer Mountain during this event. The first person prayed for was a lady with a broken leg. Without any physical touch, her leg began to shake uncontrollably as the Holy Spirit performed a 'spiritual operation'. As she cast aside her crutches and moon boot, the miracle was apparent for all to see. The scene had been set a little earlier when a guest Gospel Choir sang the powerful song *Sin's Power over me is broken* (written by T.B. Joshua). There was deliverance, healing and a manifestation of God's power as they sang.

Following swiftly on from the Emmanuel TV UK Revival, there was the memorable outdoor event in Nazareth, Israel - the land where Jesus Christ walked amongst the people, the historic homeland of the patriarchs of the Old Testament. This was the land of the Bible,

where religious pilgrims would come from all over the world for special tours, but large open-air events using that mighty name of Jesus Christ did not usually take place.

"Let the name of Jesus be glorified in His historic hometown, Nazareth, Israel - a public outdoor event on Mount Precipice so all the city may be aware."

This was an instruction from God for T.B. Joshua. Mount Precipice in Nazareth is noted in the Bible for a particular reason. It was where (as told in Luke 4) a mob, angered by the words of Jesus, tried to throw him from the top, but He passed through them unharmed.

Although many people visit Mount Precipice, the

amphitheatre there was becoming derelict and needed repair. As T.B. Joshua walked around the disused facility on a previous visit, the Holy Spirit directed him to help financially with some significant renovation for this holy site so that even after the event, the city of Nazareth would be left with a valuable renovated space.

The Nazareth Meeting with T.B. Joshua, 2019

Before June 2019, extensive renovation work was being carried out, and good relationships were being built with the local Government officials. However, anything close to Jesus faces attack, and in the homeland of Jesus, this was no exception. The story of some of the challenges faced before the Nazareth event's successful fulfilment will be discussed in the next chapter.

The age of miracles has not passed; the Miracle Worker, Jesus, is still alive! For those whose lives are centred on Jesus Christ, the best is always yet to come!

LIFE IS A BATTLEFIELD

Sitting on the plane for my first visit to Nigeria in 2001, I (Gary) was about to experience the world of gossip, innuendo and false witness. A well-dressed lady leaned forward,

"Excuse me, but I overheard you talking; you don't mean you are going to… that place?"

"Sorry, ma'am, I don't understand."

"If we were not in the air, I would have advised you to get off this plane!"

Her voice trembled with emotion and dropped to a significant whisper,

"That place, The Synagogue! You do know that his power is from witchcraft, don't you? I advise you to change your plans. His power is from the 'other side.'"

Immediately like a clear clarion call, a verse sprang into mind; was this not what the Pharisees said about Jesus? I pulled out my Bible and began to read.

"Now when the Pharisees heard it they said, 'This fellow does not cast out demons except by Beelzebub, the ruler of the demons.'" (Matthew 12:24)

ANYTHING CLOSE TO JESUS RECEIVES ATTACK

From the earliest days, we experienced negative as well as positive input about T.B. Joshua and The SCOAN but decided to seek the truth from God.

"Woe to you when all men speak well of you, for so did their fathers to the false prophets." (Luke 6:26)

All effective ministries seeking to make Jesus Christ known, to preach the Gospel and to see the Kingdom of God increase, face misunderstanding, attack and hatred. The type of attack will vary according to the customs of the time and the accusers' norms and perceptions. These change throughout the centuries and differ from one culture to another.

However, Jesus reminds us that opposition is normal,

"If you were of the world, the world would love its own. Yet because you are not of the world, but I chose you out of the world, therefore the world hates you. Remember the word that I said to you, 'A servant is not greater than his master.' If they persecuted Me, they will also persecute you." (John 15:19-20)

The Gospel of John, chapter 7 verse 12 offers a glimpse of the controversy surrounding Jesus Christ and even now continues to this day!

"Among the crowds there was widespread whispering about him. Some said, "He is a good man." Others replied, 'No, he deceives the people.'" (NIV)

Let us take a journey back to when Jesus, as a man, walked on this earth amongst people like ourselves, the educated and the uneducated, those from different religions and no religion.

"Have you heard this man Jesus?" one of the Pharisees asked. His neighbour was quick to reply. "Yes, but same as usual, it is just an emotional stirring up of the crowd. I don't believe any of it is true. What miracle? One can always bribe some poor soul to say he has received a miracle. We know what the Scriptures say, that our beloved Messiah, when he comes…" his tone lowered, reverently, "…he will come from Bethlehem as our noble Prophet Micah has instructed us. I have heard this fellow hails from the Galilee, from Nazareth, and since when has anything good come from Nazareth?"

"You are right, my friend, but the people are really taken with him," was the concerned reply.

"Don't worry, my brother, the Sanhedrin (Jewish court) will deal with him!"

And so it was to be. The Sanhedrin did indeed deal with Jesus, called the Christ, and Christianity began with the nailing of a man on a cross, waiting until his body had expired.

But there was great significance in the shedding of Jesus Christ's blood. As the Bible explains,

"Without the shedding of blood there is no forgiveness." (Hebrews 9:22, NIV)

And as T.B. Joshua said,

> "The blood Jesus Christ shed on the cross of Calvary is the most precious commodity in the history of mankind."

Of course, many who watched Him die in the flesh on the cross also witnessed His resurrection!

As accusations were hurled at our Saviour, Jesus Christ, and as they have continued to be throughout Christan history, T.B. Joshua is one of many in a long line of faithful believers who have had their characters maligned and have endured physical imprisonment, smear campaigns and false accusations.

It is clear from studying the Bible and Christian history to see that people can have difficulties understanding and appreciating the way and manner God Almighty works in the lives of different Christian believers. This is true whether they be Bishops, Pastors, Priests,

Ministers, Prophets, Mystics, Monks, Nuns or notable humanitarians and applies across denominational divides.

Christian believers whose godly life and influence have stood the test of time and outlasted their physical lifetimes appear to have several common characteristics, whether Protestant, Catholic, Orthodox, Charismatic, Methodist, Baptist, Reformed, Pentecostal, Adventist or others.

What are these characteristics?

- The Bible was their 'Book of books'; they lived in 'the Word';
- They lived a consecrated (set apart) life;
- Their lives show evidence of having an independent mind, a mind that finds out the truth from God alone;
- Humility is evident in them.

LEAVE IT FOR GOD

T.B. Joshua said on many occasions that the way and manner God works in people's lives differ. God may instruct 'Pastor A' this way and 'Pastor B' another way. One minister may have a deep relationship with God, and another may have a deeper one. Fleshly comparisons of 'ministers of God' are dangerous and tend to depend greatly upon our culture and 'worldview', that is, the lens through which we perceive and hence pronounce an instant value judgement.

The Bible is clear that it is God who will judge those who claim to be His servants. As the Apostle Paul put it,

"Who are you to judge someone else's servant? To their own master, servants stand or fall." (Romans 14:4, NIV)

He applied this principle to his own life, as well as to others,

"This, then, is how you ought to regard us: as servants of Christ and as those entrusted with the mysteries God has revealed. Now it is required that those who have been given a trust must prove faithful. I care very

little if I am judged by you or by any human court; indeed, I do not even judge myself. My conscience is clear, but that does not make me innocent. It is the Lord who judges me. Therefore judge nothing before the appointed time; wait until the Lord comes. He will bring to light what is hidden in darkness and will expose the motives of the heart. At that time each will receive their praise from God." (1 Corinthians 4:1-5, NIV)

As T.B. Joshua said, "The servants of God, large and small - God will judge."

Gamaliel spoke in the book of Acts 5:38-39 at a time of controversy over the ministry of Peter and the other apostles in Jerusalem, and his advice is as pertinent now as it was 2000 years ago,

"Therefore, in the present case I advise you: Leave these men alone! Let them go! For if their purpose or activity is of human origin, it will fail. But if it is from God, you will not be able to stop these men; you will only find yourselves fighting against God." (NIV)

Demos Shakarian was a farmer and founder of the Full Gospel Businessmen's Fellowship. His story is told in the book *The Happiest People on Earth*, which recounts how, in the days of big tent revivals in the USA in the late 1940s, he had an encounter with an evangelist who seemed to have an issue with greed. On the last night of the campaign, this evangelist, who asked people to give especially generously for the final meeting, was discovered preparing to abscond with all the offerings.[19]

Demos wants to stop him, pauses, and like a flash of inspiration in his mind, he recalls the time David crept up on Saul in the cave but decided out of respect for God not to harm Saul as God's anointed one but to leave him for God (1 Samuel 24:10).

He hears a voice he hardly recognises as his own, saying, "Don't touch him" to the ushers, who wanted to stop the evangelist. Addressing him while he was busy stuffing dollar bills into a large brown satchel,

---

19 Shakarian, D., Sherrill, J.L. and Sherrill, E. (1975). *The Happiest People on Earth*. Chosen Books. pp. 103-105

Demos said, "God does not supply His money by these methods; I do not believe God will bless it." Within six years, the errant evangelist appeared at his farm as he describes it "gaunt, unshaven and shabbily dressed". He was asking for money. Some three years later, Demos heard that he had passed away.

Why does this story matter? It is about the position of God in our lives. The Bible shows us that God is aware of what we do both in public and secretly.

"Understand you senseless among the people; and you fools, when will you be wise? He who planted the ear, shall He not hear, He who formed the eye, shall He not see? He who instructs nations, shall He not correct. He who teaches man knowledge? The Lord knows the thoughts of man, that they are futile." (Psalm 94:8)

Leave it for God! Indeed we have to be especially careful not to speak against the work of the Holy Spirit (Matthew 12:32).

Were You There When They Crucified the Lord?

As we open the portal of history, it is easy to believe we would not be like those who did not recognise Jesus Christ, but realistically this is not the case. Jesus takes time to remind the learned of His day that although they built the tombs of the prophets to honour them, they would have been the ones persecuting them if they had been alive at that time. This account is found in Luke 11:47-48. They were not happy to be told this.

Then Peter, in his famous sermon in Acts 2:36, gives a strong message,

*"Therefore let all the house of Israel know assuredly that God has made this Jesus, **whom you crucified**, both Lord and Christ."* (Emphasis added)

What would we have done if we had been part of the crowd in Jerusalem around the year 30 AD? The reality is that we would have probably gone with the majority, who, having welcomed Jesus Christ with palm fronds crying, "Hosanna!", a few days later demanded from Pilate, "Crucify Him!" Pilate, on another stressful day trying to govern this problematic region, literally 'washed his hands' of the matter and took the expedient route of satisfying the crowd and keeping the religious leaders onside. Even Peter, one of Jesus' closest associates, denied Him when the goings got too tough.

These courses of action were not taken out of a conviction that Jesus Christ deserved death, but rather out of the absence of a sufficiently strong conviction to stand against the majority when the potential personal cost of doing so was high.

We still recall some lines from a Christian folk song of the 1970s,

> *Did you join in when they started to sing*
> *Crucify, crucify Him?*
> *I know it was you for I was there too*
> *When the world said 'No!'*[20]

CHRISTIAN CONTROVERSY

More recent examples can be found in controversial ministers of God, who during their lifetimes experienced equal measures of those who believed God was using them mightily and those who thought quite the opposite. One such minister of God was Smith Wigglesworth (1859-1947) from England, known as the 'Apostle of faith'. After his death, his story has appeared in the popular Roberts Liardon book *God's Generals*, and it became possible to find his sermons widely available in Christian bookshops. He is better known now than when he was alive. Many considered him an awkward and controversial figure in his day, and there was often some stigma attached to attending his meetings.

Differences in doctrinal matters and practice amongst believers were and are the order of the day. Make no mistake about it; that is the message of history. If we are not careful, heroes of the past can be

---

20   Graham Kendrick. Copyright © 1974 Make Way Music

seen through an idealistic haze or judged as if they had operated in today's culture. The heroes of today can all too readily be ignored, misunderstood and criticised during their lifetimes.

John G Lake (1870-1935) is still both criticised and revered today. He endured accusations of practising medicine without a licence, and the undoubted miracles in his ministry were undermined by proclaiming him a 'quack' and charlatan.

Charles Finney (1792-1875), known as the 'Prince of evangelists', inspired Billy Graham and a host of others. He was controversial and attracted smear campaigns, yet he is remembered for inspiring what became known as the Second Great Awakening in the USA and the use of the 'penitent bench' during his meetings. G. Frederick Wright, who worked with Charles Finney for 30 years, recalls how a particular time of revival was marred by bitter denominational arguing (in this case, about the baptism of new believers). This almost had the effect of abruptly stopping the beautiful work of God taking place. Charles Finney's meetings attracted much criticism and orchestrated campaigns of calumny, but of those who criticised, some were later to change their views and marvel.

Rees Howells (1879-1950) is revered today by believers worldwide as an example of a righteous man, imbued with the Spirit of God, who undertook a ministry of intercession during the Second World War. His prayers are credited as Elijah of old as being 'powerful and effective'. However, he publicly predicted that the war (WW2) would end in 1940 when the opposite was the case, and it was just starting. The Press portrayed it as a failure, which turned public opinion against him and the Welsh Bible college he founded. This did not deter this godly man from Wales, and he took up the call to spiritual warfare in prayer with even more determination, knowing that God has something to say in all situations.[21]

In 18th Century Britain, theological controversy was rife. Against

---

21   Ruscoe, D.M. (2003). *The Intercession Of Rees Howells*. Lutterworth Press.

this background, one of the fiercest attacks against John Wesley (1703-1791) was a theological one. The so-called 'Minutes Controversy' (referring to the minutes from one of Wesley's conferences) raged from 1770 to 1775. John Wesley was accused of 'dreadful heresy' which was 'injurious to the very fundamental principles of Christianity,' and ordered by many prominent ministers to recant what was recorded in his minutes of August 1770. He was expanding on something he had said in 1744, "We have leaned too much toward Calvinism," for example, stating:

> Does not talking of a justified or sanctified state tend to mislead men? Almost naturally leading them to trust in what was done in one moment? Whereas we are every hour and every moment pleasing or displeasing to God, according to our works: according to the whole of our inward tempers and our outward behaviour.[22]

For this expression of 'practical Christianity', his name was blackened, and many turned against him.

And so we come to T.B. Joshua - Prophet, Pastor, Teacher, Humanitarian, Father in the Lord to many - and The Synagogue, Church Of All Nations.

For over two decades, we have had a 'front-row seat' and the opportunity to observe the depth of the efforts to stop this mighty ministry from moving forward. From the earliest times of our involvement with this 'move of God', we have received no shortage of negative opinion from far and wide about T.B. Joshua and have been introduced to the world of false witness and accusations, smear campaigns, evil attacks and character assassination.

"Life is not fun and games. It is a battlefield where only the serious-minded are victorious." (see 2 Timothy 2:3-4).

Anyone seeking truth needs patience and an independent mind and should consider the character and track record of the man T.B.

---

22   Fletcher, J. (1795). *First check to Antinomianism... G.* Paramore. p. 7

Joshua in uplifting the name of Jesus Christ in signs, wonders and miracles of healing. This has been consistent for over 30 years. There are multitudes of examples, many video-recorded for posterity. Also, there is the profound Bible teaching and constant encouragement to listeners to make God's Word their standard for lives and their daily meditation.

Matthew 7:18: explains, *"A good tree cannot bear bad fruit, nor can a bad tree bear good fruit."*

There is no neutral kingdom! The blackness of the human heart without God and the hatred of Christ and the Christian Gospel are real. The rage against God is observed daily in the Western world. The book of Genesis reminds us that in Noah's days (as today),

"...every inclination of the thoughts of the human heart was only evil all the time." (Genesis 6:5, NIV)

The Prophet Jeremiah proclaimed the same truth,

"The heart is deceitful above all things, and desperately wicked; who can know it?" (Jeremiah 17:9)

C.S. Lewis (a 20th-century Professor and theologian) echoes this,

"We never find out the strength of the evil impulse inside us until we try to fight it."[23]

FALSE TESTIMONY

The Ten Commandments are a set of Biblical principles relating to ethics and worship that play a fundamental role in Judaism and Christianity. For centuries, they have shaped Western Christian democracies, providing rules for civil life for the religious and non-religious alike. Children used to be taught the Ten Commandments in Sunday Schools alongside the Lord's Prayer as basic tenets of the Christian faith.

---

23   Lewis, C.S. (1952). *Mere Christianity*. Macmillan. p. 78

The ninth of those commandments is this: "You shall NOT bear false witness".

Like many other sinful behaviours, false witness, or false testimony, is the natural product of a corrupt heart,

"For out of the heart come evil thoughts—murder, adultery, sexual immorality, theft, false testimony, slander." (Matthew 15:19)

All it needs is for bitterness or offence to take root in the heart, and all their evil companions - including false testimony - emerge.

In Christian history, false claims, smear campaigns, slanderous remarks, libellous writings and concerted campaigns of calumny have been plentiful. This should not surprise us, as our enemy, satan, does not want to see the Gospel prosper. And satan will mercilessly use every kind of human weakness for his ends before dropping his instruments and leaving them in misery.

"For we do not wrestle against flesh and blood, but against principalities, against powers, against the rulers of the darkness of this age, against spiritual hosts of wickedness in the heavenly places." (Ephesians 6:12)

False accusation is rampant, like the other 'sins of the heart' such as lust and anger. It can be a simple, effective strategy used by the evil one to bring down a Minister or ministry. The issue is not necessarily the accusations themselves but the effect of sowing seeds of doubt into hearts. These seeds of doubt can then germinate and grow, removing believers from their glorious destiny to an offended cynical, weary lifestyle where religious services become a duty.

From the Scriptures, we observe that when we believe a lie, we don't just regress to a neutral position; we are in danger of becoming an evangelist to spread gossip, rumours and lies to distort the truth. Anyone can be Peter; anyone can be Judas! Offence and lying can be endemic. Psalm 12:2 reminds us that,

"Everyone lies to their neighbour; they flatter with their lips but harbour deception in their hearts."

Proverbs 6:16-19 instructs us that,

"There are six things that the Lord hates, seven that are an abomination to him: haughty eyes, a lying tongue, and hands that shed innocent blood, a heart that devises wicked plans, feet that make haste to run to evil, a false witness who breathes out lies, and one who sows discord among brothers."

Offence, hatred, bitterness, envy, jealousy, poverty and desire for money or notoriety can drive many to subvert the truth. We have seen this in action. The truth does not change, but people can and do change their 'story' depending upon what they aim to achieve at a certain point in time. We were to witness this on different occasions.

This was also made apparent in a completely different context to Fiona when completing her duty to undertake Jury service in the UK.

We 12 jurors drawn from the multicultural UK received a stern lecture from the judge before we would start to consider the evidence, following a serious accusation. The judge explained that people lie for many reasons and also cry and show emotion even when lying. It was a complex case, and the stories at first seemed quite convincing but began to carry less weight as the trial wore on. In the end, 10 out of the 12 jurors were ready to pronounce their judgment of 'Not Guilty'.

In the political world, smear campaigns are simply part of a political armoury before a campaign. In the vernacular, 'If you throw enough mud at a person, some of it will stick and be believed.'

Some campaigns are planned to remove a person from this earth. Naboth's Vineyard is one such account in the Bible. 1 Kings 21 verses 9 to 14 has the story of Jezebel and her deliberate use of false accusation to take the life of an innocent man,

"She wrote in the letters, saying, 'Proclaim a fast, and seat Naboth with high honour among the people; and seat two men, scoundrels, before him to bear witness against him, saying, "You have blasphemed God and the king." Then take him out, and stone him, that he may die.' So the men of his city, the elders and nobles who were inhabitants of his city, did as Jezebel had sent to them, as it was written in the letters which she had sent to

them. They proclaimed a fast, and seated Naboth with high honour among the people. And two men, scoundrels, came in and sat before him; and the scoundrels witnessed against him, against Naboth, in the presence of the people, saying, 'Naboth has blasphemed God and the king!' Then they took him outside the city and stoned him with stones, so that he died. Then they sent to Jezebel, saying, "Naboth has been stoned and is dead."

When Nehemiah was under instruction from God to build Jerusalem's walls, several nefarious attempts were made to get him to leave the job. One of Nehemiah's responses was to refuse to engage with the 'supposed' reports because, as Nehemiah 6 verse 9 says, *"they were trying to make us afraid and weaken the work."*

At the end of the work, the Bible notes that the enemies perceived that this work was done by God.

The persecution of T.B. Joshua in Nigeria was also beyond the ordinary. The level of colourful and vitriolic accusations over the years against the ministry in an extensive collection of print media and online websites would beggar belief. There would be prayer meetings and rituals to stop the ministry, and locals would be persuaded to spread lies and hold placards outside the church protesting.

Whilst all this 'noise' was going on, we were calmly taking groups to The SCOAN. The most consistent testimonies were that visitors would draw closer to God and return to their countries to be more active members of their various local churches.

We have witnessed over the years how, in the face of a myriad of accusations, T.B. Joshua continued to keep his attention on his goal of proclaiming the good news of Jesus Christ and setting the captives free,

> It is not what men say about you that really matters in life; it is what you believe about yourself. Jesus was slandered; He was falsely accused. He never begged anyone to believe in Him. They accused Jesus of being filled with devils! Yet, He paid no attention. He simply continued to cast out devils (Matt 12:24).

People always fight what they do not understand. Throughout human history, men of God have had their names soiled and stained. Accusations and slanderous lies have come against great political leaders as well as ministers of God. This is a reality in life. Daniel, for example, was accused of breaking the law. Joseph was falsely accused of raping his employer's wife. Knowing all these, Jesus never wasted His time with His critics. He simply kept His attention on His goal.[24]

TV INTEREST TURNS SOUR

Early on, there was some international interest from broadcasters in what was happening at The SCOAN, especially the healing. However, The SCOAN is not an ordinary place and one's motive matters. The Holy Spirit exposes true motives, and here is one such example, so 'ridiculous' that it bears examination to understand what lies behind it.

In the early days before Emmanuel TV, a TV crew from a UK independent production company were given permission to visit and record parts of a service and various interviews. They had said they were working for the BBC, and during the visit, they were very complimentary, even giving positive live visitor experience interviews during the service. However, this all turned out to be misleading. Although the programme's working title was said to be "Worldwide Christianity", the final result was broadcast on Channel 4 in June 2004 under the title "God is Black".

We watched incredulously as the programme portrayed simple conversations in the local language (Yoruba) by local evangelists as sinister, and an interview with T.B. Joshua was edited in a very misleading way. Even shots of the prayer line had scary music overlaid in the background.

At that point, there was no presence in the UK, no Emmanuel TV,

---

24   T.B. Joshua, *To Know The Truth is to Know Jesus Christ*, SCOAN leaflet, available in 2001.

no international Gospel events and yet, here was a clear attempt to smear the ministry in the UK.

On another occasion, when there were some regular meetings for prayer in the UK, some undercover reporters showed medical reports for serious conditions, pretending they were desperate and asking for prayer.

"Please, will you help me? I want prayer for xxx condition", the young woman clasped her hands beseechingly, her dark eyes looking at us imploringly. "I have been attending for four weeks; why can't you pray for me? Here is my medical report." The team were getting ready for one of the regular meetings for prayer with the Anointing Water.

Prayer for the sick has been part of the Christian liturgy from New Testament times, although the way and manner it is offered vary across Christian traditions. Perhaps more importantly, the success of the prayer offered 'in the name of Jesus Christ' may depend on faith both in the one praying and the one receiving. However, it is widely accepted and therefore consummately strange that such a service open to the public without any suggestion of money being involved and in daytime hours should receive undercover media attention.

Why were we sure something was wrong with the woman's story? It can only have been the Holy Spirit warning us that what we saw on the outside was not the whole story. We explained that it was not yet the right time to pray for her; little did we know that the woman was trying to set us up so her undercover camera team would see her receiving prayer and be free to make their allegations. Frustrated by our refusal, a wildly inaccurate story was published anyway (including Fiona's picture) in the online version of a well-known newspaper.

Later, the news media raided a Sunday morning service with their cameras forcing their way past the ushers. We had no idea what they expected to see! It was not a large meeting, and the service had already finished, allowing time for a nice cup of tea together and chat, and the team were attending to visitors.

The majority of attendees had already left when the broadcast news team pushed their way in. They approached a team member with their camera and microphone and demanded to know why we were discouraging certain patients from taking medication (which was not true). She informed them we would be happy to schedule a meeting with them but needed to finish attending to the people there. They persisted in trying to get a comment but didn't get anywhere. We thought they had probably made a mistake in the timing and were hoping to burst in midway through the service. One team member tried to block them by putting her hand in front of the camera, thus providing a clip that they eventually used in the broadcast to support their utterly unfounded narrative.

12 SEPTEMBER 2014

On 12 September 2014, we returned home from a friendly visit to a SCOAN Scholarship student at Oxford University to the news that there had been a major incident at The SCOAN in Lagos. A building that housed international visitors had suddenly fallen in on itself, and there appeared to be many casualties. "The greatest trial since the beginning of my calling" was how T.B.Joshua would describe this tragedy.

This was not the only international disaster that had taken place that same year, where it was not immediately clear what had actually happened. For example, there were two Malaysia Airlines aircraft that crashed – one lost over the South China Sea and the other shot down over eastern Ukraine. When such serious incidents occur on the international stage, it is common for different observers to expound theories of what may have happened. Social media are typically buzzing with suggestions, some far-fetched and others more plausible. However, official sources close to the incident are usually more cautious and advise waiting until official investigations have been carried out before reaching conclusions.

However, in the case of the SCOAN incident, local Government officials were immediately quoted as prejudging what had happened without examining or even being aware of the evidence. They appeared to lend support to a campaign that saw news reach other countries the same afternoon, already portraying T.B. Joshua as the villain of the piece. Nothing could be further from the truth, but the smear campaign persisted. It seems as if there was a specific campaign to go to the Press with attacks on the ministry. One of the narratives was that church people were unhelpful to the rescue operations. In contrast, in giving actual evidence, the Nigerian Red Cross said the opposite,

> The church authorities were good and helpful to us. They were so passionate about the rescue operations. And I can tell you categorically that they never stopped us from doing our job. Rather, their efforts really covered our inadequacies.[25]

The actual moment of the building collapse was caught on CCTV security cameras, showing the whole building falling in on itself symmetrically and completely in just under 4 seconds, without affecting adjacent buildings.

CCTV Footage Showing the Whole Building Collapsing Symmetrically

The nature of the collapse clearly points not to any structural failure but to controlled demolition, or "building implosion", of the kind employed to demolish unwanted buildings without affecting adjacent plots. Mr Derrick Garvey, a South African architect with more than 50 years of experience, was unequivocal when speaking about the incident on South African National TV, "When the building falls in on itself in a cloud of dust, it cannot be anything else... It was an imploded controlled demolition. There is

25 *Synagogue Building Collapse: Witnesses Vindicate Church as Coroner Allays fears of Prosecution*, The Maravi Post, 30 Oct 2014

absolutely no doubt about that."[26]

Such a demolition needs to be meticulously planned to ensure that the building falls within its own footprint. Typically small and strategically placed explosives are employed, although hydraulic pumps can also be used, and with appropriate planning and preparation, other techniques could trigger an implosion.

The CCTV images and video recorded by eyewitnesses also clearly show that a low-flying aircraft was close to the building, circling it four times on the morning of the collapse. This aircraft was clearly visible as a Hercules C130 owned by the Nigerian Air Force. The authorities officially acknowledged this, but no explanation or details were given, except that it was "on a circuit training mission". We had visited The SCOAN dozens of times and had spent many months living there and had never seen any such aircraft before.

The presence of this plane in the area uniquely on that morning just minutes before the implosion is indisputable even if there may not be any direct evidence of what the aircraft was doing.

There are different theories. For example, an academic article from July 2015 postulates that the SCOAN building destruction was likely to be triggered by an infrasonic weapon carried on the aircraft.[27] A different private article explains how a chemical laser could have been employed from the plane to trigger explosives that caused the implosion.[28]

In two articles published in June 2017, a former Minister of Culture and Tourism and Minister of Aviation of Nigeria argues that the SCOAN building was blown up in a secret operation conducted by rogue elements in the intelligence agencies. The author claims to have been told this by operatives working within the agencies and

26   *Newsroom, 31 July 2015*. SABC News YouTube Channel, 31 July 2015
27   Iguniwei, P. B. (2015). *Elimination of the Structural Failure and the Placement of Chemical Explosives Options...* International Journal of Scientific Engineering and Research 3 (7).
28   *A Thorough Examination Of The SCOAN Building collapse, debunking some theories*, The Maravi Post, 23 Oct 2014

explains in some detail the possible political and religious motivations for such an attack.[29,30] Whether or not this is a plausible explanation or a conspiracy theory, we know for sure that the ultimate conspirator, satan, had wanted to destroy the ministry of T.B. Joshua.

MAINTAINING FOCUS UNDER PRESSURE AND TENSION

The response of a prophet, a 'God's General' of our time, to the challenge that faced the ministry in 2014 at the time of the building collapse was instructive, and we had the privilege to see that response in action.

Let us take a step back and examine the situation as it unfolded.

There had been an extraordinary event in Colombia, with the Olympic Stadium filled. T.B. Joshua was planning to come down from the mountain where he had been staying in rustic accommodation to pray before the stadium event and move to a place where he could be more accessible for visitors to meet him.

But then the warning from God: "A cloud is covering Nigeria. Return to the Prayer Mountain (home in Nigeria) and pray. And one more thing, purchase a new CCTV system for the land in Ikotun Egbe."

This was July, and the instruction was followed. On Friday 12 September, the day of the 'attack', the man of God was praying at the Prayer Mountain when reports came in of a strange plane circling The SCOAN.

This evil attack was treated as such by the calm example of the man of God.

"Broken focus is the real reason men fail."

---

29 *Femi Fani-Kayode: How TB Joshua's church building was bombed [Part 1]*, Daily Post, 5 Jun 2017
30 *Femi Fani-Kayode: How TB Joshua's church building was bombed [Part 2]*, Daily Post, 7 Jun 2017

Even in the midst of this agonising trial, his focus did not change. Preventing any panic ensuing, he was calmly organising the evangelists in rescue teams using the ambulances present 'prophetically' on-site. He continued in an attitude of prayer at all times. Whilst there were many martyrs that day, there were also many rescued to tell their unique stories.

During the Sunday service following the fateful Friday, the man of God was to be seen with unchanged focus standing strong for all those watching on Emmanuel TV and those physically present in the church. The prayer line continued, and this was during the time the rescue events were continuing successfully for those trapped under rubble.

We arrived in The SCOAN just one week after the incident and were able to see the unswerving focus in action.

We had the privilege to join a team headed to South Africa to meet those who had lost family members in this attack. They were people of faith, humble and prepared to take the hard things of life in faith. The love enkindled in people's hearts for the ministry was awe-inspiring, spiritual, of Heaven. History will reveal what shall come from the lives of these martyrs - people who met an unexpected death in pursuit of God. They and their families have set an example, a standard of behaviour that we can only hope to emulate. Many families would continue to be supported by the ministry through education.

Crusade with T.B. Joshua in Mexico, 2015

Fast forward to Mexico 2015. As we gazed around the packed Aztec stadium (the largest in Latin America) and saw the name of Jesus Christ honoured and lifted high, a few short months after that devastating attack, we thanked God that His servant Prophet T.B. Joshua's focus had not been broken. Many of the families of the martyrs were present as guests of honour.

The evil attack, for such it was, was intended to disable and mortally wound the ministry. But to God be the glory, as the time has passed, whilst there are still mysteries to be finally resolved in God's time, the ministry has come out stronger.

NOISE IN NAZARETH

In June 2019, T.B. Joshua held a historic meeting on Mount Precipice in Nazareth, Israel, the hometown of Jesus Christ. 1000s travelled from around the world. However, before the event took place, there was noise throughout Israel to the extent that they said the event would be cancelled.[31]

Religious leaders from both Christian and Islamic traditions appeared on TV to warn their followers,

"Even out of curiosity, [our people] should not go; if they do, they would be promoting a liar, a person who doesn't like the benefits of the Christian faith. This man is only promoting lies, and anyone who follows this liar is unjust. That is why we ban our people from indulging in this event."

"We should not give this place, which is considered to be highly holy, to a wizard. We should not allow him to use our land to advertise

himself. I am against this visit; this person is provoking people of all religions in Nazareth. They should ban him and not give him any opportunity at all!"

"Boycotting the sorcerer zionist is a national and religious duty."

Before the event, Mount Precipice was even set ablaze to stop the event from occurring. A protest also took place, the people chanting, "Listen to us! Let this witch get away from us! Mount Precipice

---

31   *Persecution is Promotion! Lessons From TB Joshua In Nazareth,* TB Joshua Ministries Facebook Post, 21 Aug 2020

will never be humiliated by you, coward!"

The noise continued even as the event was taking place. As T.B. Joshua preached about love, religious groups opposite the meeting broadcast this message: "Do not participate with this wizard. This is a witch in our decent land."

Even after the event, a group of religious people performed a 'ritual' at Mount Precipice, claiming they were cleansing the Biblical site using salt, water and leaves.

T.B. Joshua continued nevertheless until he finished what the Lord had sent him to do in Nazareth, calling the name of Jesus Christ in public there after 2000 years. Not only that, healing, deliverance, signs and wonders took place in His name.

"So they called them and commanded them not to speak at all nor teach in the name of Jesus. But Peter and John answered and said to them, 'Whether it is right in the sight of God to listen to you more than to God, you judge'" (Acts 4:18-19)

As T.B. Joshua said about this event,

> You only need to hear, 'Go!' from above, from Heaven. Who are you to say no? When God says yes, no man can say no. The noise of north and south, the noise of east and west, does not matter. It only promotes.[32]

We had the privilege to observe all of this unfolding before our eyes. Indeed, even from a planning and organisation point of view, the event frequently looked as though it wouldn't be able to go ahead. But Prophet T.B. Joshua had heard the word from Jesus saying 'Go!' As he explained to one of the team members questioning whether the event really could go ahead, as far as he was concerned, it had already happened in Heaven. We simply needed to hold our ground in faith.

---

32   Ibid.

YOUTUBE SUSPENSION

By 2021, Emmanuel TV had become the most-watched general Christian channel on YouTube, with its videos translated into multiple languages and collectively viewed over 1,000,000,000 times. However, in April 2021, YouTube shut the channel down, citing its Community Guidelines which prohibit "hate speech".

Many subscribers expressed their shock and surprise by flooding social media with requests for YouTube to restore Emmanuel TV on its platform. Some made known their distaste for the decision in articles for the African press. For example, one piece complained, referring to YouTube,

> They claim their actions were based on 'hate speech' from a deliverance video. A video which to a true believer is an inspiring testimony of transformation.[33]

Other commentators raised concerns about the wider implications for all who might hold to conservative Christian values. For example, Noah Pitcher, the Global Politics writer for Today News Africa, a US-based international news organisation focused on US-Africa policy, reflected that,

> The label of hate speech can feel loosely defined, all-encompassing, and open to subjective interpretation... This raises many concerns amongst religious communities about whether pastors can be punished for merely reading the teachings of Scripture.[34]

The Nigerian-American Press Association also weighed in, describing the decision by Google (the parent company of YouTube) as "discriminatory".[35]

Against this background of potential tension and conflict, T.B. Joshua

33   *The Tyranny of Social Media Giants and Modern Persecution of the Church*, The Maravi Post, 17 Apr 2021
34   *YouTube walks dangerous line between tolerance and censorship in its decision to terminate channel of famed Nigerian pastor T.B. Joshua*, Today News Africa, 21 Apr 2021
35   *YouTube ban was 'work of God' – TB Joshua*, The Nation (Nigeria), 19 Apr 2021

addressed the issue directly at an Emmanuel TV Partners' gathering, encouraging supporters to appreciate and to pray for YouTube,

> What happened is a blessing. I want you to help me pray for YouTube. Pray for them! Don't see them the other way around; see them as friends. We need to be strong.
>
> Humanly, I know the way you look at it is not the way I am going to look at it. I look at it differently. Remember to pray for YouTube. Many of you who are here today - if not for YouTube, you may likely not be here. It was through YouTube you viewed T.B. Joshua and were able to come here. Please, pray for them. Look at it in another way.[36]

He went on to explain that, as Christians, whatever we are going through is to prepare us for the future. What matters is not what one party or the other is saying, but what the future says. We must take every response to God in prayer.

Again, Prophet T.B. Joshua did not lose his focus on his relationship with God. As Apostle Peter said,

"Those who suffer according to God's will should commit themselves to their faithful Creator and continue to do good." (1 Peter 4:19, NIV)

Free Advertising

T.B. Joshua never advertised his sermons or church services yet managed to attract worldwide attention. The secret? Persecution!

> Let people advertise you. Don't fight. If truly you are genuine, whatever people say about you – whether they condemn you, spoil your name or praise you – it is for your good.[37]

John Fletcher, a close colleague of John Wesley - himself no stranger to dealing with controversial issues - nearly 300 years ago, made a similar observation, reflecting deeply on how satan's opposition turns out to work for the good of the Gospel,

---

36 *My Response to Emmanuel TV's Suspension on YouTube*, TB Joshua Ministries Facebook Post, 18 Apr 2021
37 Official TB Joshua Twitter Account, 18 Apr 2017

The more the god of this degenerate world exalts himself in opposition to truth, the more he disposes every sincere heart for the reception of it. The Gospel is that everlasting rock upon which the Church is founded, and against which the gates of hell can never prevail; and though this rock is assailed by innumerable hosts of visible and invisible enemies, yet their repeated assaults serve only to demonstrate, with increasing certainty, its unshaken firmness and absolute impenetrability.

A clear sight of the sovereign good, as presented to us in the Gospel, is sufficient to make it universally desirable. The veil of inattention, however, conceals, in a great measure, this sovereign good, and the mists of prejudice entirely obscure it. But by the inhuman conduct of the persecutors of Christianity, their false accusations, their secret plots, and their unexampled cruelty, these mists are frequently dissipated, and these veils rent in twain from the top to the bottom.

Error is by these means unwittingly exposed to the view of the world; while every impartial observer, attracted by the charms of persecuted truth, examines into its nature, acknowledges its excellence, and at length triumphs in the possession of that inestimable pearl which he once despised. Thus the tears of the faithful, and the blood of confessors, have been generally found to scatter and nourish the seed of the kingdom.[38]

COMMITMENT ENHANCES FAITH

"Active faith makes those things that are against us to be for us."

Indeed those things that are intended to come against the people of God can work for their advancement. Faith must be tested in a real situation. When you stand on your commitment throughout testing, Jesus will give you more faith.

This chapter finishes with the words of a powerful sermon by T.B. Joshua, explaining why persecution is inevitable and revealing the profound relationship between faith and commitment.

---

38 Fletcher, J. (1804). *The Portrait of St. Paul.* Kirk & Robinson. pp. 116-7

COMMITMENT ENHANCES FAITH

T. B. Joshua, The SCOAN Sunday Service, 12 August 2018

John 15:18-19 – *If the world hates you, keep in mind that it hated me first. If you belonged to the world, it would love you as its own. As it is, you do not belong to the world, but I have chosen you out of the world.*

The world hates the disciples of Jesus, and you are one of the disciples. If you are a follower of Jesus, though you are in the world, you are not part of it. That is why the world hates you – because you are not part of everything the world stands for. There is a barrier between us and everything in the world if you are a disciple.

The instant, the moment, we become identified with Jesus Christ and accept Him as our Lord and Saviour genuinely, the world will hate us. The evidence that you receive Jesus truly, genuinely, is that the world will hate you. The world currently under satanic control will hate you in the same manner that it hates Jesus.

Some of us would say, "Why should we suffer and die after Jesus won the victory on the cross and suffered for us?" The answer is found in John 15:20, where Jesus said,

"A servant is not greater than his master. If they persecuted Me, they will persecute you also."

Anybody who claims that he does not have to suffer because Jesus suffered for him is contradicting what Jesus said. In other words, we are saying that when we accept Jesus Christ as our Lord and Saviour, we are accepting citizenship in Heaven and death here on earth. Total commitment is what Jesus demands throughout the Gospel.

The doctrine that says there will be no suffering, no health challenges, no hardship is not in line with God's Word because a man can be sick in body and yet be a candidate of Heaven, a friend of Jesus. A man can be poor and yet be a favourite of Heaven.

Don't allow your situation to rule you. Many today, when they are sick, begin to see Jesus in a bad light. There are both good and hard times alike in our walk with the Lord, when the goings are good and when things go the other way. We learn best when things are going the other way rather than when things are going our way.

We cannot separate warfare from salvation. True salvation will put us into direct conflict with satan. The day you make a total commitment to Jesus, you have declared war against satan. By identifying yourself with Jesus of Nazareth, you have made yourself a bitter enemy of satan.

Once Jesus purchases us, we become aliens here on earth – strangers. There will be a barrier between us and everything here on earth. What is the barrier? You cannot go where Jesus will not be welcomed; you cannot say what Jesus would not want to hear; you must go where He will be welcomed.

Before you can be accepted, commitment asks Jesus to accept you. You say, "Lord Jesus, I am a sinner. Wash me with Your precious blood; save my soul," and you stop smoking, going to nightclubs, fighting and living with jealousy. However, until your heart accepts what you are saying, you are not such in heart.

Commitment asks Jesus to accept you.

There are many things you have done or claim you are doing, but you are not such in heart. For example, you accepted Jesus as your Lord and Saviour, and you stopped smoking, but you are still smoking in your dreams. You live a restricted life; you are not free; that is, you always live with urges – urge for this and that. You say, "I am a child of God", but you find yourself drinking alcohol or sleeping with different women in your dreams. That is because you are not such in heart.

Commitment stands as a bridge, a go-between, a link, an intermediary, between us and Jesus. Commitment means, "mean it with all your heart". The moment you make a commitment, you will be tested and tried to show that you really mean what you are saying. Are you real, or are you deceiving yourself?

When you stand on your commitment throughout testing, Jesus will give you more and more faith as you go along. Faith is a pure gift from God. You cannot grow in faith if you do not make a commitment. Only faith pleases God.

If you are a Christian, a believer, a pastor, a bishop, a prophet, or if you are about to be, in every step, a suggestion must come to you from the Spirit that the action be performed. I am a servant. I cannot dictate the kind of direction, position, or what to say; I cannot decide what suffering to bear.

You iron your clothes and say you will wear this on Monday and that on Tuesday – how do you know that you will live to see those days when you are an alien, a servant, a stranger here on earth? That is one of the big insults we give to God.

What is the position of God? The day you wake up and say, "Next, I do not know. Over to you, God," then you are a Christian, a follower of God. The fear of God will be there.

We own now; God owns our future. You take over now; He takes over your future. You can start it now. Leave your 'next' for God.

GOD CAN USE ANY MEDIUM

"Anoint Water! This Anointing Water will go to places difficult to reach!" Such was the instruction received from God. It was an instruction in righteousness that came out of T.B. Joshua seeking the face of Almighty God at the Prayer Mountain and as such was bathed in fervent effective prayer.

ANOINTING WATER

In the period between the first set of International Gospel events (crusades) in different countries up to 2007 and the second set of such events, which began again in 2014, there was the launch of the 'Anointing Water', sometimes known as 'Morning Water'. Starting in larger bottles, soon the bottles would be reduced in size to ones that could be officially carried on a plane.

Why Water? Well, God can use any medium, and as T.B. Joshua pointed out, you can apply water safely to different parts of the body.

This instruction's effect was immense; for example, the Anointing Water freely given to visitors to The SCOAN would feature in testimonies from all around the world, representing different languages, cultures, time zones, and Christian experiences.

This free gift was controversial to some people and entirely acceptable to other parts of Christendom.

These areas are mysterious. For example, the Anointing Water is, in one sense (chemically), ordinary water. Yet, in another sense, how could it be ordinary? It did not come out of a board meeting discussion with numbers and quotas and prices and timescales, and the anointing behind it is authentic and powerful.

COMMISSIONED TO TRAVEL

As evangelists for the glorious Gospel of our Lord and Saviour Jesus Christ and under the direction of Prophet T.B. Joshua, there came a time when we were sent far and wide across the world to preach the Gospel and pray for the sick and afflicted in the name of Jesus Christ using the medium of the Anointing Water.

It was the beginning of October 2010, and we were visiting The SCOAN in Lagos. It had been a difficult time when the various attacks against the ministry had been noisy in our country, and we made a request to come and pray to seek God's face in such a place of faith.

It was great to be there, yet interesting because we were waiting and we did not know what we were waiting for! We tried to be patient, but it was a time of testing. In private conversation between ourselves, we recalled the occasions five and six years previously when we had visited Russia to encourage the believers there and help some visit The SCOAN, and how much we had enjoyed meeting the Russian believers.

Just before we were due to leave for the airport, we received a call to come to the office. What happened next was as if it was straight from the Bible,

"One of his servants said, None, my lord O king; but Elisha, the prophet who is in Israel, tells the king of Israel the words that you speak in your bedchamber." (2 Kings 6:11-13)

We entered the small office, aware that this was a meeting with a prophet. We believe to this day that T.B. Joshua did not know what he was going to say to us when we entered the office. Slowly, he took a bag with bottles of Anointing Water, paused, waited, seeming (to our rapt observation) to be listening, and then filled it until there were 11 or 12. And then it came, the instruction in righteousness:

"You people are evangelists. Go to Russia! Let me pray for you."

Slowly, deliberately, he joined our hands together, held them and prayed, "Father, commit Yourself to their protection, strengthen their desire for Christ." It was a sending, a commissioning, to "show what the water can do". Faith, peace and an immense sense of purpose flooded our hearts, and even at Lagos Airport waiting to board, we started our research into how to 'make it happen'.

What followed was to launch us into two years of itinerant travelling, mainly to Russian-speaking countries.

Across the cold, remote wastelands of Asian Russia, to the edges of Uzbekistan, to small one-bedroom apartments in Kazan with 50 people crammed in, to hidden Christian meeting places in Karaganda in the vast 'steppes' that comprise Kazakhstan, the believers, often still meeting somewhat secretly, had heard of T.B. Joshua, and wanted to experience the anointing of God.

The meetings, be they large or small, would follow a similar format: a time of preaching from the Gospels, often based around Blind Bartimaeus (Mark 10:46-52), the Canaanite Woman (Matthew 15:21-28) or the man let down through the roof (Mark 2:1-12). This was to help the congregation focus on Jesus and be asking for His mercy. We would then show videos (with Russian translation) of testimonies with prayer using the Anointing Water and of mass prayer from The SCOAN. The congregation would stand and join in the mass prayer, and this would nearly always result in some people manifesting evil spirits and then proclaiming healing.

It was also an opportunity to explain that there was no particular theology connected to water and that the Anointing Water was not for sale: God can anoint anything, and one cannot sell 'anointing'. T.B. Joshua himself explained that any payment for the water, or even for its postage or delivery, would make it 'ordinary water'. Many believers in different countries from different walks of life, particularly those who were poor, understood this very simply.

Reactions to Prayer with Anointing Water

It was in one such remote place, with the snow falling freely, that we saw the raw power of God, beyond culture, beyond race, beyond comfort. The congregation came forward and waited expectantly in a line. The water was sprayed without a human touch. No sooner had those words, "In the mighty name of Jesus Christ!" been spoken than people began screaming, crying, and lunging again and again. The transition from standing neatly and politely to exhibiting anger, rage and even animal-like behaviour with sinister noises was instantaneous.

One such lady, repeatedly lunging at us and growling while we were praying and spraying the water, would be the one the following day to testify of a remarkable improvement in her physical health.

"The thief does not come except to steal, and to kill, and to destroy. I have come that they may have life, and that they may have it more abundantly." (John 10:10)

SOME TESTIMONIES

It would be difficult to quantify the number of times we saw or heard follow-up testimonies after prayer spraying this water. We personally experienced God's protection and significant improvement in our physical condition when we experienced health challenges during our travels.

KYRGYZSTAN

Healing in Kyrgyzstan

Outstanding memories include the healing of a lady with a dislocated and cracked knee at a large church meeting in Kyrgyzstan. She arrived for the prayer registration using crutches, unable to put any weight on the injured leg, and we took a full interview. We encouraged her to remain in faith, and she was seated at the back of the hall. We explained that we would go to her during the ministry time to spray the water, believing God for Him to reduce her pain. What happened was amazing. Jesus came on the scene; she appeared to fall almost into a trance and then stood up joyfully and confidently and walked down the stairs without her crutches and onto the stage. After that, she wanted the bandages and cast removed, and a local nurse obliged!

UKRAINE

Then, there were the testimonies of those who received 'fruit of the womb', having been childless for many years. On one visit to a church in Ukraine in September 2012, we had the joy of recording three 'miracle baby' testimonies at the same time. For a while, there was a special Anointing Water designated by Prophet T.B. Joshua as being for the fruit of the womb, and this featured in each of the testimonies.

One woman had been diagnosed with a large ovarian cyst, and the doctors had advised her that she was unable to conceive. Her medical reports and scans clearly displayed the large cyst. We had prayed for her in Jesus' name using the Anointing Water in a service in Ukraine at the end of 2010. We had also given her a bottle of the special 'Fruit of the Womb' Anointing Water to use at home. Three months later, she conceived, and by September 2012, her healthy daughter was nine months old.

Another couple also received their miracle through the ministration of Anointing Water but in a different way. The church pastor had returned from a visit to

'Fruit of the Womb' Testimonies in Ukraine

The SCOAN at the beginning of March 2011, bringing some of the 'Fruit of the Womb' Anointing Water with him. Inspired by what he had witnessed at The SCOAN, he held a 'fruit of the womb' prayer service in his church, passing round a scarf he had anointed with the water. The child was conceived just one month after that prayer of faith.

The third couple were the pastors themselves. Having been trying unsuccessfully for a second child, their first child now 18 years old, they also prayed with the Anointing Water brought back from Pastor Dima's visit to The SCOAN. They found that within a month, they too were expecting a baby.

Another Ukraine Testimony

Pastor Dima revisited The SCOAN in November 2011 to share their testimony and also to seek God for a breakthrough in supernatural ministry for the whole church. He received a prophecy from T.B. Joshua during the service, explaining how God would use him in his nation. Then, when he met with T.B. Joshua at the end of his visit, he received an impartation where he felt the power of God descend into his hands. There was indeed a spiritual breakthrough in his church on his return.

PAKISTAN

A Russian Pastor connected us with a church in Pakistan, where we also took the Anointing Water. Here, the testimonies extended to the rural farming communities. Rev. Khalid Jamali sent us this testimony after one of our visits,

> I went to the village of Chathian Wala, buffalo herders live there. Everyone has 10 to 30 buffaloes but one woman has only one buffalo. She has only the earning source of one buffalo and that buffalo was near to death that time when we were there for a meeting of anointing water. The lady came and I gave her anointing water. When the buffalo drank it, after two minutes the buffalo was well, and the woman started crying with happiness and joy.[39]

The following year, we were able to visit that village and record some other testimonies from the use of the Anointing Water, including the story of a young man called Zahid. His family income was derived from a wheat field just outside the village, which insects had spoiled. They couldn't afford to spray the area with insecticide, but with faith in the

Farming Testimony in Pakistan

blood of Jesus Christ, they sprayed the field with Anointing Water. The wheat grew, and that year they harvested a record crop.

In the densely populated inner-city neighbourhood of Kahna Nau in Lahore, Pakistan, we followed the pastor through a doorway to a shabby yard, where we saw a young man stretched on a mattress.

---

39   Private email communication, 4 Sep 2012

The man called Shahzad looked up at us. We were shocked to hear he had been lying down for months with a severe anal wound that worsened by the week.

Gary quickly sprayed some Anointing Water on the wound, we also sprayed some in a bottle of his own water to use later, and we encouraged him to remain in faith in Jesus Christ.

Returning six months later, we listened to his incredible testimony spoken in Urdu.

Healing Testimony in Pakistan

"I had a wound on my buttocks for seven months. I couldn't go to the washroom. All the time, I lay on my bed. I prayed to God to help me. Last year, you came with Anointing Water from T.B. Joshua, and brother Gary sprayed some of it on my wound. A few days later, it healed up completely. Everything in my life, I am now doing normally. I received my healing through this Anointing Water, through the power of our Lord Jesus Christ."

SOME ADVENTURES

In the middle of our journeying throughout the former Soviet Union to Khabarovsk near China's borders, we were to experience an unusual attack. T.B. Joshua often reminded the church that, as believers, there is no 'time off'. We need Jesus in every area of our lives at all times.

"Be sober, be vigilant; because your adversary the devil walks about like a roaring lion, seeking whom he may devour." (1 Peter 5:8)

The night before, we had prayed for many with the Anointing Water and seen some dramatic deliverance cases. We returned to the pastor's accommodation to rest before our long journey. Russian Christian hospitality is famous, and taking us to the airport, the pastor was keen to be sure we ate well. The local restaurant had a star attraction, a large angry bear in a cage that we were shortly to discover was not secure at all. Our host wanted us to pose for a picture, and reluctantly we agreed. Fiona explains what happened next,

The Angry Russian Bear

Suddenly I see Gary staggering, and instinctively I pull him away (just in time). The cage is not in good repair, and the bear has put his teeth deep into Gary's arm through his coat (an evil attack aimed to cut his arm off, as a South African hunter friend later explained). This was Gary's arm, so used for the Gospel in all the translation work, post-production editing of charity recordings etc., not to mention spraying with the Anointing Water. The wound was deep, blood was flowing, and I got out the Anointing Water and quickly sprayed the arm. On medical examination, the wound was found too deep for suturing; it had to be dressed regularly. The scar is still present on Gary's arm. It was indeed an evil attack!

There would prove to be some interesting reactions to the Anointing Water from those who had invited us in to pray. At the end of a long air journey to what felt like the other side of the world lies the former penal colony of Sakhalin Island between the Asian Russian mainland and Japan. As we prepared for the meeting, we realised a somewhat animated discussion was going on in the next room between the pastor and others leaders. 'What about this water? Is God really using it? Is it theologically sound?' It was touch and go whether we would be allowed to pray with the water, but, thank God, we were able to explain that it was 'all about Jesus' - the water just being a symbol to help people's faith - and they gave us the benefit of the doubt.

A Russian Gospel singer from the US had been invited to lead the same guest service. He was not told about us nor we about him. The pastor had 'double-booked'. We were able to see the funny side of this, and indeed God was in control. The Gospel singer proved to be most helpful, and he got thoroughly involved in the ministry, acting as translator for some of the great testimonies. The following day, together with the pastor who had stood his ground about the ministration of the Anointing Water, we all went to the beach in the snow. We recorded them as they gave warm Christmas greetings to the Emmanuel TV viewers.

At a small meeting in Ukraine, our translator was an imposing gentleman with a flowing black beard. He first greeted us warmly, but as the point in the service came where we showed the explanatory video about anointed water, which we showed everywhere we went, he reacted strangely. Sitting at the front, he got up dramatically as the footage showed T.B. Joshua demonstrating prayer for healing using the water, glared at us and walked out. We never saw him again. What happened? It was indeed a spiritual response to the work of God on the screen. The host pastor did not speak English, but one of the team arranging the meeting had some command of the English language, and she stepped in as though nothing had happened.

The meeting proceeded and ended with Raisa, an elderly babushka (grandmother) who had come to the service using a walking stick, throwing away her stick and riding away happily on a bicycle!

At a meeting in the UK, there was a calm lady of impeccable manners. We knew because we had spent an hour with her as she shared her concerns about her child; she appeared the nicest possible lady. Fast forward to the prayer line, and with one spray of the Anointing

Water and the mention of the name above all names, Jesus Christ, we were facing a different person. Screaming, she reacted back and let forth a long tirade of foul language and perverse accusations, "You wicked fornicator, I know all about you". Screaming and shouting, the woman advanced determinedly. What was happening? It was time for the prayer line, and the medium used by the Holy Spirit to separate light from the darkness was the Anointing Water. The lady was wonderfully delivered from that demon that had been tormenting her and her family.

OTHER ANOINTING WATER TESTIMONIES

Testimonies of God's work through the Anointing Water would become a regular feature of the live SCOAN services on Emmanuel TV. One young man from the USA (a country suffering excesses of opioid and alcohol deaths) described his story with a dramatic reenactment shown on Emmanuel TV.

As a young man faced with life's vicissitudes, job loss, unhappy childhood memories, poverty and failed relationships, Chris began drinking heavily and overdosing on pills. He was to end up in the

Joining in with the Mass Prayer Remotely

Emergency Room and was fortunate even to be alive. Then a new start; he was introduced to Emmanuel TV and began to watch the Bible teaching and join in with the mass prayer during the live services.

What happened next? Chris explains,

> I met an evangelist from The SCOAN. She gave me a bottle of the New Morning Water by Prophet T.B. Joshua. When I got home, I began to minister it to myself and apply it to myself every day, believing God for healing and deliverance. And I got that healing. A couple of months later, I was able to throw out

all the pills. It's been almost six years now that I have taken medication. Now, I feel free and good. I used to be depressed and suicidal. Now, I work with all kinds of kids that grew up in hardship just like I did. We feed the homeless, help the elderly, and do all kinds of great things. I am just so thankful and grateful that God used Prophet T.B. Joshua to bring the Morning Water into my life and heal and deliver me. If God can do it for me, He can do it for you.[40]

Some 'New Anointing Water' was released in January 2021 to traverse the world. Emmanuel TV partners worldwide would receive this New Anointing Water as a free gift and minister it, often through video calls on phones, to the sick in other countries following the example of faith. Soon the testimonies would be crowding in, and the faith of an ever-increasing number of people would be strengthened - not to mention the many lives healed, delivered and blessed.

Encouraged by T.B. Joshua holding the New Anointing Water at Prayer Mountain, and excitedly watching the video testimonies pouring in from different countries, some Emmanuel TV partners put their faith to work. They sprayed the water on the phone screen during a call with a woman in another Russian-speaking country who was rapidly losing weight and energy. Every time she ate normal food, she experienced severe allergic reactions.

The prayer session was recorded, so the reaction was for all to see. Manifesting and falling on the floor, the urge to 'vomit something out' was irresistible.

Healing Testimony from Crimea

Standing up and wiping her mouth, Tatiana from Crimea knew something had happened. Emboldened, she prepared a typical meal of vegetables and fish, the first for many

---

40   As broadcast on Emmanuel TV during 2020. Confirmed by personal communication

weeks, and, praise the Lord, experienced no adverse reactions. She continued to eat normally and enjoyed walking once again.

'FRUIT OF THE WOMB' MEETINGS

During one of our extended periods of living at The SCOAN, there were two large 'Fruit of the Womb' meetings. On 5 December 2008, the auditorium was filled with potentially expectant couples and those already 'with child' who had come for prayer for safe delivery.

One hopeful couple, Mr Pieter and his wife from South Africa with a documented history of long-term infertility, were among the international visitors. They had received prayer, but before moving on, T.B. Joshua first walked towards the ornamental container in front of the altar area. This held fresh fruit, placed there before every service day. Taking some of this 'anointed fruit', he gave it to the couple to encourage their faith.

Testimony Following the 2008 Fruit of the Womb Service at The SCOAN

Travelling back to their home country, they conceived naturally and were delighted to announce their pregnancy. All proceeded well, and they welcomed their beautiful baby boy before 2009 was finished. In 2010 they visited to show their baby to all and were also accompanied by other family members. On his first visit to The SCOAN, the little one was to be seen contentedly observing the Sunday service as his parents publicly gave glory to God for this glorious answer to prayer.

The 2009 Fruit of the Womb gathering began with a time devoted to hearing the testimonies from the previous year and seeing the miracle babies within their mother's arms. It was also noteworthy as T.B. Joshua was to be seen wearing a large scarf (a mantle). He passed the mantle from person to person; some reacted strangely and even fell to the floor; many returned in the coming months with their testimonies of answered prayer following that encounter. Indeed we saw that God could use any medium.

Anointed Objects in the Bible

Upon earnest prayer and a genuine desire for the anointing on his life to reach more people, T.B. Joshua made use of different 'anointed objects' over more than 25 years.

The object is not the important thing but the anointing. Our experience in using these anointed objects over the years has taught us to appreciate that "The fervent effective prayers of a righteous man avail much" (James 5.16), rather than pointing to any new theology. The power of God we experienced, for example, in prayer with the Anointing Water on the other side of the world from Nigeria was to show us time and again that it was no different from the handkerchiefs sent out by Apostle Paul (Acts 19:11).

God can use any medium:

- In Acts 19:11-12, God used the medium of Paul's handkerchief and aprons to heal the sick.
- In Exodus 14:16, God used the medium of Moses' staff to split the Red Sea.
- In Acts 3:6, God used the voice of His servants, Peter and John, to raise a crippled man.
- In 2 Kings 5:14, God used the medium of a dirty river to heal Namaan.
- In Acts 2:1-2, God expressed Himself through the medium of sound at the time of Pentecost

- In 1 Samuel 17:49, God used David's catapult to defeat the giant Goliath.

- In John 9:6-7, Jesus used mud and saliva to heal a blind man.

- In Acts 5:15-16, God used the medium of Peter's shadow to heal the sick.

Before the introduction of the Anointing Water, the ministry had already used, for example, sand, water taps, fragrant oil, anointed handkerchiefs, keyrings with scriptures, stickers, sermon notes and the altar area in the church sanctuary as 'points of contact' to help people's faith.

One of those, keyrings with scriptures written on them, provided Fiona with a powerful testimony.

The keyring was in the small car I was driving when it was hit by a huge truck on 31 January 2003, the day before I was to take a small group to visit The SCOAN. I only remember the car flying up in the air, turning over three times and being set down almost gently on the outer lane of a busy motorway. I had to be cut out of the car by the Emergency Services but was not injured (except for a few bruises), and no one else was hurt.

There would be a frequent stream of similar testimonies of God's protection from car accidents with the Anointing Water in particular.

One early video that was shown regularly to visitors to The SCOAN showed a situation where one of the weekly church sermon notes served as an anointed object. A mother with her newly-delivered baby that was apparently lifeless arrived at The SCOAN in a taxi. When the sermon note was placed on the tiny body, one could see the glow of warm live flesh appearing as the baby came to life.

Then subsequently there have been other 'points of contact': Taps to dispense 'living water' on the church altar, faith bracelets, the 'Believers Card', touching the screen during the live broadcast of Mass Prayer within Sunday services and on online video clips, as well as the traditional 'laying on of hands' by T.B. Joshua and other ministers of God in training at The SCOAN. More recently, interactive prayer 'at a distance' from the Emmanuel TV studios has followed.

Were all these things controversial? Of course, but that tended to be when too much attention was given to the object being anointed. As the booklet that was given to visitors to accompany the Anointing / Morning Water said,

> The Anointing Water is just a symbol, not the power itself. It is not the water that heals, delivers, blesses and saves but God Almighty Himself since the anointing is done in His name.

> Before ministering the Anointing Water, there must be faith both in the person praying and in the person being prayed for.

Evangelist Bill Subritzky from New Zealand was one of the early foreign visitors to The SCOAN. He took a group of ministers there to see the power of God and to reach a decision from an independent mind. At that time, there was a monthly service known as the 'Blood of Jesus' service, where Prophet T.B. Joshua would pray and then anoint some water taps and the water coming out of them, and people would come to touch or drink the water believing for a miracle.

In response to various theological criticisms he had received about this phenomenon, he wrote:

> The evidence of their belief comes in their immediate deliverances from demon power. This belief in the power of the blood of Jesus is similar to that exercised by those upon whom aprons were laid after touching the body of Paul. Because of the power of the blood, the demons left the people and they were healed. It is clear from scripture that God in his grace and mercy can use inanimate objects such as prayer cloths and water for deliverance and healing. We see evidence of this in the touching of the coffin by Jesus whereby the widow's son was raised from the dead. We see it in the power on His garment and the power in the waters of Bethesda. There was power in the clay that Jesus put on the blind person's eye and there was power in His spittle when he placed it on the blind

person's eye. There was power in the waters of the Jordan when Naaman was healed. Similarly, there was power in the bones of the deceased Elisha when the dead person touching them was brought to life. There was power in the mantle of Elijah and there was power in the hair of Samson. There was power also in the rod of Moses when it was turned into a serpent. There was power in the rod of Aaron when he touched the dust and it turned to lice.[41]

We have seen that indeed the use of anointed objects, and particularly the Anointing Water, enabled the anointing of God on the life of T.B. Joshua to reach many more people and places than would otherwise have been possible. It has also given those who minister the water in healing and deliverance to others some experience of 'working with the Holy Spirit' to potentially help them grow to receive and maintain more anointing themselves.

A.A. ALLEN'S SIGNATURE STAMP

During our time of itinerant travelling and meetings in America, we were privileged to meet with a Grandpa of faith, an elderly healing evangelist C.S. Upthegrove, whose ministry spanned over 55 years. He had worked closely with many of the renowned healing evangelists of 1950s America, especially A.A. Allen with his church in Miracle Valley. Introduced to the ministry by his daughter, he began to watch Emmanuel TV. Astonished at what he saw, he subsequently accepted an invitation from T.B. Joshua to make the long journey to Africa (a continent he had never visited) to visit The SCOAN.

In the course of that visit, there were two notable occasions for this 'living legend' to teach from his long experience and wisdom of God's work in his life. C.S. Upthegrove would explain about a 'God's General' of the past, A.A. Allen, who received so many prayer requests and wanted to reply to them all personally, so he had made a personal signature stamp. Explaining further, he told all those in

the church and watching on Emmanuel TV,

> When it was presented to me, I said, "The Spirit of the Lord is still in that stamp". God can use anything, I told you – he can use sticks and stones, dead men's bones; he uses water. He uses shadows, and He used this stamp in the hands of A.A. Allen. And when it was passed to me, I treasured this, and I kept it. My children said, 'Leave it to us, dad.' I said, 'No, this is not for the inheritance of the children. This is to pass on to another prophet of God.'[42]

The years passed. Still, the signature stamp remained in his possession until this moment when reverently C.S. Upthegrove passed it to Prophet T.B. Joshua during the live Sunday service on Easter Sunday, 8 April 2012.

He described how A.A. Allen had prophesied to him before his death,

C.S. Upthegrove Presents the Signature Stamp of A.A. Allen to T.B. Joshua

> I was riding one day in the automobile with A.A. Allen, and he looked over at me, and he said, 'Brother Upthegrove, I may not be living when this comes to pass, but I believe you will'. And he began to describe this place. He began to talk about a man that would walk out under the anointing and the power of the Almighty God. He further described all of the miracles I have witnessed since I have been here.[43]

Indeed, preaching dynamically, one could see his strength visibly increasing as he encouraged all present to live above fear, doubt, condemnation, and unbelief. Later, in a full-length interview with a team of evangelists, he would give a riveting account of all his experiences in the work of the Lord and once more express his delight at meeting T.B. Joshua in his lifetime.

---

42 *God's General CS Upthegrove Visits Prophet TB Joshua SCOAN.* CS Upthegrove YouTube Channel, 11 Sep 2013
43 Ibid.

THE POWER SOURCE

This power of God is not to be exercised at will; it is under the instruction of the Holy Spirit, the third person of the Trinity. God uses 'suitable' people who are available to God in His way, not our way.

There is a mystery to the way the Holy Spirit works. However, there is evidence of a 'deeper' relationship with God, in that T.B. Joshua spent much of his life in prayer to maintain the anointing he received from God, surrounded by nature at the Prayer Mountain. He would often say, 'I give myself to prayer' (Psalm 109:4).

The water, and any other anointed objects, would be kept by the altar with the prayer warriors at Prayer Mountain, bathed and saturated in prayer.

Many people would come to The SCOAN searching for power or anointing for their ministries. They would indeed receive an impartation, but maintaining any impartation requires more commitment, devotion and dedication. As Prophet T.B. Joshua explained to a group of visiting foreign pastors back in the year 2000,

> Everyone can receive the Holy Spirit, but God is looking at your future. The issue is to maintain. It is better not to receive the Holy Spirit than to receive and then lose it.
>
> Have you prepared every area of your life for the Holy Spirit?
>
> To maintain the anointing, go into a covenant with God to be humble and obedient and faithful to the letter forever. It is between you and God. We need to be more committed to God; we need to be more serious.[44]

He has also explained that we must be grounded in the Word of God, the Bible, before receiving the anointing of the Holy Spirit,

> I meet a lot of people expressing the desire to be Spirit-filled; I applaud that desire, but there is a problem. The major problem is that you must be grounded in the Word before you are

---

44 *The Holy Spirit*, Divine Lecture 4 VHS tape, SCOAN, 2000

Spirit-filled, else there will be nothing there for the Spirit to remind you of - you will be empty.[45]

If you want to live in the Spirit, keep in the Word, abide in the Word; become totally saturated with the Scripture, and you will find yourself overflowing with the Spirit.[46]

There is power in the name of Jesus! That name can cause the demonic forces to recoil and flee, but only when exercised in the right way.

"The name of Jesus Christ has power indeed, but only among those who are committed to the glory of God. "

Prayer and too quick a use of 'laying on of hands' can become a dangerous mission, as illustrated clearly in this passage from the Bible:

"Then some of the itinerant Jewish exorcists took it upon themselves to call the name of the Lord Jesus over those who had evil spirits, saying, "We exorcise you by the Jesus whom Paul preaches." Also there were seven sons of Sceva, a Jewish chief priest, who did so. And the evil spirit answered and said, "Jesus I know, and Paul I know; but who are you?" Then the man in whom the evil spirit was leaped on them, overpowered them, and prevailed against them, so that they fled out of that house naked and wounded. This became known both to all Jews and Greeks dwelling in Ephesus; and fear fell on them all, and the name of the Lord Jesus was magnified." (Acts 19:11-17)

T.B. Joshua explains that the seven sons of Sceva are examples for us of those who profess affinity or closeness to Christ according to the flesh, while remaining unchanged in heart and life. Things can go well up to a point, but then one day the "stiff opposition" will come - *"Jesus I know, and I know about Paul, but who are you?"* meaning, "By what authority? What authority have you to command us? Who gave you such authority? What right have you to declare the

---

45   *Power from Above*, SCOAN Sermon Note (MPG) based on Sunday sermon of 3 Apr 2016
46   How to be filled with the Holy Spirit, T.B. Joshua, 9 Sep 2018, Sunday Service

authority of Jesus, seeing that you disobey His instructions?"

So we learn that the name of Jesus only truly has authority on our lips when it is also planted in our heart.

Understanding these realities led us to shift our understanding of Christian theology away from our previous 'modern charismatic' standpoint. For example, we saw that one should not separate the fruits and gifts of the Holy Spirit. The popular illustration of the gifts of the Holy Spirit being like gifts hung on a Christmas tree, and the fruits like fruit growing on a fruit tree, is unhelpful. Rather, the fruits are everything. A supernatural gift may look the same externally, but if accompanied by the fruits of the flesh, it is from satan, and if accompanied by the fruits of the Holy Spirit, it is from the Holy Spirit.

THE EXAMPLE OF APOSTLE PAUL

"The book of Acts is not mere history; it is the pattern of what Christ wants His church to be today."

In the book of Acts, we are told the story in some detail of a controversial Apostle. This is not the Saint Paul of famous Basilicas in Rome, or beautiful religious paintings in museums in Western Europe, of feast days and even of the well known treatise on love in the book of 1 Corinthians read at so many weddings. This is the 'raw' Paul, who explained that *"signs and wonders were done amongst you with great perseverance"* (2 Corinthians 12:12). He did not have a mega-church, and many people spoke against his ministry. At the end of his life, this disciple of Jesus, who describes himself as one born 'out of time', was still a controversial character, frequently deserted by the believers and spoken against. In 2 Timothy 1:15, Paul says, *"You know that everyone in the province of Asia has deserted me."*

There were false accusations hurled at Paul, including a specific charge that he had brought Greeks (Gentiles) into the temple and defiled it. The Jewish believers in Jerusalem encouraged Paul to fulfil some traditional aspects of the Jewish religion, which were expected to dispel any rumours against him by being ceremonially clean in the temple. Still, despite that, there were false accusations that he had defiled the temple by taking a Greek Gentile believer inside. This false accusation is referred to many times. In Acts 24, Paul is being hauled up by the authorities before a ruler called Felix. Facing allegations and a death penalty, he calmly remarks, referring to Jesus Christ,

"But this I confess to you, that according to the Way which they call a sect, so I worship the God of my fathers" (verse 14)

Verses 5 and 6 give us a sample of how false accusations were made against him,

"For we have found this man a plague, a creator of dissension among all the Jews throughout the world, and a ringleader of the sect of the Naza-renes. He even tried to profane the temple, and we seized him."

Apostle Paul knew from the start of his revelation of Jesus Christ that he would be suffering for Him. Imprisoned in Rome, he was a condemned man, waiting for the martyrdom that would surely come. Paul, the book of Acts tells us, sought to use the then Scrip-tures (what Christians now know as the Old Testament) to persuade the Jews in Rome who visited him to hear his defence. When he arrived under house arrest in Rome, where he was to spend the last years of his life under sentence of death, the Jews came to hear him because, as it says in Acts 28:22,

"...concerning this sect, we know that it is spoken against everywhere".

This controversial believer who had his radical encounter with Jesus Christ on the road to Damascus, as we understand, was eventually beheaded under the Christian persecution in Rome.

This was not the end of the story. Apostle Paul had written the famous letters which have become part of the Canon of Scripture. Fourteen of the twenty-seven books in the New Testament have traditionally been attributed to Paul. Today, these epistles (letters)

continue to be vital roots of theology, worship and pastoral life throughout the Christian traditions.

However, it was three centuries after Paul's death, at the Synod of Hippo in 393 AD, that the anointing upon Apostle Paul's teaching was formally recognised by including these epistles in the Canon of Scripture. It is easy for us now looking back to see the significance of Paul's writings, but it was not so obvious at the time.

Acts 19:11-12 tells us that,

"God worked unusual miracles by the hands of Paul, so that even handkerchiefs or aprons were brought from his body to the sick, and the diseases left them and the evil spirits went out of them."

So as well as the controversy and persecution, the way God used anointed objects that the Apostle had touched is a similarity we can see between his ministry and that of Prophet T.B. Joshua.

Apostle Paul had different instructions from the Holy Spirit than the Jerusalem apostles, and this did, the Bible tells us, cause conflict and misunderstanding. The message of the Gospel needed to go to the Gentiles, but at the time, many followers of 'The Way' were only focusing on Jewish believers.

As we peer down the corridors of time, we are thankful that Apostle Paul chose not to be defined by his culture and upbringing but was obedient to the Holy Commission.

T.B. Joshua said,

> "What people do not understand, they call names; what they understand, they destroy. I pray people will not understand you."

THE BIBLE AND THE HOLY SPIRIT

It is essential to have a spiritual understanding of the Bible. It is unlike any other book. T.B. Joshua explained that anyone can enter a bookshop with some money and buy a Bible, but the holiness contained in the Bible is not for sale. And the Bible is not to be understood in the same way as a Chemistry or History textbook. It is necessary to approach the reading of the Word of God with a humble and sincere heart.

This chapter ends with the following sermon, explaining more fully the vital relationship between the Bible and the Holy Spirit.

READ THE BIBLE, READ THE HOLY SPIRIT

T. B. Joshua, The SCOAN Sunday Service, 1 July 2018

2 Peter 1:20-21 – *"Above all, you must understand that no prophecy of Scripture came about by the prophet's own interpretation of things. For prophecy never had its origin in the human will, but prophets though human spoke from God as they were carried along by the Holy Spirit."*

As Christians, this is our standard for life – the Holy Bible. But with the way we approach the Bible today, it's easy to see we do not know the difference between the Bible and other books; we do not know the difference between the Bible and history, chemistry and literature. We just believe we must read it like every other book.

But the Bible itself is the letter inspired by the Spirit of God. As the Lord breathed His Spirit into certain men, so He breathed His Spirit into certain books. Therefore when you are reading the Bible, you are reading the Holy Spirit

Holy men were carried along by the Spirit of God as they spoke the message that came from God. If you must read the Bible, you must be carried along by the Holy Spirit. When we pray and read without any attention or regard for the Holy Spirit, we do not place Him where He rightly belongs, knowing how important He is to us. When you read without the attention of the Holy Spirit, it makes no meaning to you because you are reading history, events, what happened in Jerusalem, what happened to Jeremiah, what happened to Jesus Christ.

The Holy Spirit is the most sensitive of beings and is easily hurt by lack of attention and regard. God is Spirit, and His worshippers must worship Him in spirit and in truth. Before reading the Bible, we must seek the attention of the Holy Spirit because the Bible is the tool in the hands of the Holy Spirit.

God speaks to us through His Word, by His Spirit. He calls you through His Word, by His Spirit. He whispers to you through His Word, by His Spirit. He greets you through His Word, by His Spirit.

Romans 9:1 – *"I speak the truth in Christ, I am not lying, my conscience confirms it through the Holy Spirit."*

This means that the Holy Spirit is a communicator, and our heart is the contact point. The Holy Spirit cannot communicate with a heart full of bitterness, unforgiveness, hatred or bad feelings towards others. You can read the Bible 100 times, but as long as you hold grudges against anyone, the Bible makes no meaning to you. We are very good at reading the Bible, but God does not necessarily reward good people, clever people, smart people or wealthy people; He rewards obedient people, those who make God's Word the standard for their lives.

Can you see where your challenges and problems come from, why you cannot invite the Holy Spirit to your heart? Without the Bible, how will you get to God, have access to God or talk to God? Without the Bible, there is no Christianity, no child of God, no believer, no born again. The Bible is our standard.

Ask yourself this question, "Why does the Bible not come alive to some of us nowadays?" The Bible can no longer come alive because of the unforgiveness we hold – bitterness, envy, jealousy and bad feelings towards others. To come alive means to understand and to know what it is to read for salvation, healing, deliverance and all of

God's blessings.

How can the Bible become real to us? Read the Bible as often as possible; keep meditating on it until it becomes a reality to you; read it slowly, repeatedly and attentively; it is not like any other book. When you are reading the Bible, put your knowledge aside; your spirit must act on the Word to be part of the Word – for God's Word refreshes our mind, and God's Spirit renews our strength. Even though our reasoning may reject it, let our heart crave for it. Jesus needs your heart; that is the place of contact.

To all the hearts that are in bondage (bondage of unforgiveness, bondage of envy, bondage of jealousy), free your spirit to follow Him.

Do as Christ instructs in Matthew 5:23-24,

"Therefore if you are offering your gift at the altar and there remember that your brother or sister has something against you, leave your gift there in front of the altar. First go and be reconciled to them, then come and offer your gift."

Without the freedom, the liberty of your heart, you are calling a God you do not know, and your Bible reading has no meaning.

THE PROPHET ON THE MOUNTAIN

"*Have you not known? Have you not heard? The everlasting God, the Lord, the Creator of the ends of the earth, neither faints nor is weary. His understanding is unsearchable. He gives power to the weak, and to those who have no might He increases strength. Even the youths shall faint and be weary, and the young men shall utterly fall, but those who wait on the Lord Shall renew their strength; they shall mount up with wings like eagles, they shall run and not be weary, they shall walk and not faint.*" (Isaiah 40:28-31)

Prophet T.B. Joshua at the Prayer Mountain in Ondo State

143

Where does the power come from to see the race to the end? From waiting on the Lord. Life is a marathon, not a sprint.

Following a time of prayer at the Prayer Mountain in Ondo State close to his village, T.B. Joshua spoke to Emmanuel TV viewers from the mountain on 30 December 2020, referring to the importance of habit and of staying close to nature,

> Every rightful man simply has great habits. Habit is a gift from God. Right from the beginning of my ministry, I have been staying close to nature. Nature enhances spirituality.

> Daniel prayed three times a day on his knees (Daniel 6:10).

> The psalmist prayed seven times daily (Psalm 119:164).

> The disciples of Jesus Christ prayed on the first day of each week (Acts 20:7).

> These were their habits.

THE PRAYER MOUNTAIN

"You will have your own Prayer Mountain". Such instruction came from the encounter of Prophet T.B. Joshua with Jesus during a 40-day fast in 1987 on the physical mountain where he used to pray, close to his hometown in Ondo State.

Jungle ('bush'), raw with animal droppings, cobwebs, the caress of moist heat, huge leaves and green vegetation. Insects and birds, monkeys and toucans, tropical rain, thunderstorms, bamboo huts and simple boats. This virgin land on the outskirts of the Lagos megacity would include the first prayer hut and humble abode where the man of God, dressed in a simple white robe, would spend hours of his day and night in prayer before the Lord God, who had given him such a profound destiny. Saints and hermits of old sought the lonely places, and it was from there they would minister.

From this place close to nature, yet also close to the people, the church began in 1989. By 1994, it relocated to its present location, just under two miles away. T.B. Joshua would travel to and from the

'Old Site', now known as the Prayer Mountain, often many times a day. Indeed it was aptly named for this was indeed a 'spiritual mountain'.

He would return to the simplicity and solitude of the Prayer Mountain to be with God in nature, whether from a service at the main church auditorium with thousands of visitors from as many as 50 different countries or from one of the stadium events in other countries.

A man of prayer; this indeed was how the news of T.B. Joshua and the biblical miracles crossed the oceans. 'There is a Christian brother in Lagos, Nigeria; he lives simply in swampland in the bush. The Holy Spirit instructs him who to pray for, and he sees them in visions. They call him a prophet because he speaks accurate words from God.'

International visitors to The SCOAN would gather to climb into the bus. From their first arrival, they had asked, 'Can we go to Prayer Mountain?' The answers were enigmatic, 'As the Holy Spirit directs,' but now we were going, turning down the teeming streets with buying and selling everywhere. Walking through the wooden walkway over the bridge, we came to the jungle, water (reclaimed from the swamp), and the first 'Mercy Land' with sand. We took a small boat to the interior, saw the vastness of the external vision and caught a glimpse of the immensity of the spiritual vision.

Fiona Enjoys a Visit to Prayer Mountain in 2004

Enjoying the opportunity to go to the Prayer Mountain, the visitors would find a place on the sand and be asking for God's mercy and favour. It was not a time for loud words and cries but for the Word of God to pierce hearts and minds.

In this place, reading the Bible with an open heart, verses would leap out from the pages like fire, becoming spiritual food to be tasted and nourished, to help us back in the world of work and challenges.

Walking around as the Prayer Garden trees began to grow, all thoughts of unforgiveness would flee away. This was a mighty spiritual cathedral where the Lord's Prayer came to life.

"Give us this day our daily bread. And forgive us our debts, as we forgive our debtors. And do not lead us into temptation, but deliver us from the evil one." (Matthew 6:11-13)

PRAYER VIGILS

From the earliest times, the church members would meet at the 'Old Site' for night vigils. Among those first church members would come the first prayer warriors, those who would be living a set-apart life. They would give their time not to making a noise and saying words but to asking the Lord God of the Universe, the One who was and is and is to come, to protect and fulfil the destiny of this humble man from Arigidi, Ondo State.

Indeed we have observed that even those who clean the Prayer Mountain facilities are themselves devoted to prayer, following the example of T.B. Joshua's mother, who would pray, "Clean my life, as I clean your house". The Prayer Mountain is not an ordinary place.

As the church members would be invited and welcomed to pray, how to pray was always the question; what kind of prayer is not just 'saying words'? This was not the kind of prayer that sets out a 'shopping list' for God to fulfil, or which takes its direction from the immediate situation and its apparent needs, but rather prayer to bring our hearts in line with God's Word,

> *Take me as I am, O Lord, You can still cleanse me*
> *Because no one is too good or too bad to qualify for salvation*
> *All I need is Your mercy and favour*
> *Dirty as I am, O Lord, You can still cleanse me*

Don't comfort me until You cleanse me
Let Your mercy and favour speak for me
Create a clean heart in me and renew a faithful spirit within me

O Holy Spirit, Breathe in me, that my thoughts may all be holy
O Holy Spirit, Act in me, that my work too may be holy
O Holy Spirit, Strengthen me, to defend all that is holy
O Holy Spirit, Guide me, that I always may be holy

[song]
Prayer is the key; prayer is the key
Prayer is the master key.
Jesus started with prayer and ended with prayer.
Prayer is the master key.

T.B. Joshua would attend the Prayer Vigils, and he would walk amongst the members, often giving personal prophecies but also ones of national or international scope. We remember being at one such vigil where he said, "Our new President, he will be wearing this 'Bayelsa hat'," and he pointed to one man wearing such a hat. Months later, when President Goodluck Jonathan was elected, he was never seen without his famous hat, confirming the prophecy.

As the huge International Gospel events (crusades) were developing, locating a 'Prayer Mountain' in different countries was an integral part of the preparation. For example, in Colombia, the accommodation for T.B. Joshua was up a physical mountain with a narrow road, and there, with nature spread out in front of him and a simple rustic cabin to sleep in, the man of God would pray. The local organiser made specific reference to how this had significantly impacted him in his opening remarks at the Pastors' Conference. Never before had he met an international guest preacher who on arrival did not want to be taken to a hotel to rest but to a mountain to pray.

CALLS FROM THE MOUNTAIN

When we were travelling to pray for people with the Anointing

Water, any calls we received from our mentor were sacred and usually made from the Prayer Mountain. They were holy interactions, not business interactions. As anyone who has had the privilege to receive a phone call from him will know, these are not 'ordinary' conversations. As he revealed during a sermon, he is listening to instructions from above at the same time that he is saying, "Hello. How are you?" The man of God balances his life by taking in the life of Christ and giving it out.

One such life-changing call came at about 3 am. That night after the first services with the Anointing Water in Kazan, Russia, we were sleeping in bunk beds in a one-bedroom flat with a family of four. In the middle of the Russian night, the phone rang, "Is that Dr Gary? Hold on for the man of God". The smile in our mentor's voice reached over the miles from Africa to Russia into that room and set the scene for the rest of our journeying. He was referring to the testimonies we had sent.

"I have seen what is happening; it is wonderful. You should go from country to country and return every so often to collect more Anointing Water."

There in the tiny room, beside the bunk beds, at 3 am Russian time, we knelt on the worn rug to thank God, and the presence of the Holy Spirit filled the room. It was as though we were at the Prayer Mountain listening to a Bible teaching or in the office at the church with T.B. Joshua.

A few months later, we arrived in Rostov-on-Don to find that the pastor had gathered over 500 people, including other pastors, for a four-day healing conference. We looked at each other, slightly taken aback.

That night, we managed to get through to our mentor on the phone and simply said, "Sir, there are a lot of people here, and they are looking for healing." The response was instant,

"Jesus is with you people; it will be as if Jesus was there praying."

And indeed, it was to be. There were testimonies of people dropping walking sticks, bending their knees without pain from arthritis for the first time in years, and many others.

There is something about a word spoken from the heart, affected by the Spirit of God. The words do not just convey information but can impart faith and life. In one of his sermons, T.B. Joshua explains the two 'languages' we can use:

> There is *Bible language*, which is the language of the heart, that God uses to save us, create us, judge and rule over us. There is also the *language of today*, which we use to gossip, give direction and do politics.
>
> When we use the language of today, we don't mean what we say. But when we use Bible language, we mean it.
>
> People often use the language of today to pray, and that is why whatever they say in prayer seems not to be permanent; their prayer is mere words.
>
> But when the Word is in your heart, it will preserve you from desiring sin. We need the Word of God in our heart to bring Jesus on the scene.[47]

Teaching in the Prayer Hut

It was 2004. We sat in a small round Prayer Hut at the Prayer Mountain with a bamboo roof with our Bibles, and the door opened. To

our surprise, T.B. Joshua came and joined us. Sitting on the floor with his back to the wall, he started to talk about Daniel's example in the Old Testament. This was not a chat or a business discussion but a time of personal teaching.

A Prayer Hut at Prayer Mountain in 2004

We would refer back to our

---

47   *Faith is of Man's Heart*, T.B. Joshua, 16 Sep 2018, Sunday Service

scribbled notes made while he was talking to us many times. They proved to be prophetic. Indeed, as he would later teach in a Sunday Sermon, prophecy is not just about predicting the future but also about preaching and teaching God's Word with power (the power to change the hearers).

"This is a perilous time, a hard time, like the time of Daniel and of Shadrach, Meshach and Abednego. It's getting to the end of the world, when all the Bible says is coming to pass. But a time of crisis is a time of pleasure in the Spirit.

When the decree was published, Daniel's detractors went to see his reaction; he was still praying openly and thanking God. Daniel did not complain before going into the lion's den; he didn't murmur, fall into self-pity or cry. He had every right to fall into self-pity since he was a captive, and his father and mother were not there. But he knew that before gold becomes gold, it has to pass through the furnace.

The same with Paul and Silas: They were severely beaten and had done nothing wrong; you might have expected self-pity. They kept praying to God and came out stronger.

For Christians, God is always one step ahead. After trials proved their belief, they became statesmen. Daniel dined with kings. His relationship with God went to a new level.

Everyone has his own hard time. For example, for Mr A, it might be poverty, for Mr B sickness, for Mr C depression and for Mr D persecution - different crises. If it is the will of God for Mr A to experience poverty, he will come out stronger.

How do we know if it is the will of God? When we are follow-ing God in truth and faith, then if something happens, it is the will of God. But if we are in sin, it is not the will of God.

If you fear or you doubt in the trial, your god will become the god of fear or the god of doubt. Daniel knew God would save him; therefore, he didn't murmur. What we need God to be in a trial is what He is for us. This is what God wants us to know at this time.

There are many battles in a war. If you overcome one battle, it doesn't mean you have the complete victory. In the trial, His name is 'I am who I am' and 'the Steadfast and Trustworthy One'. God never dodges a crisis but sees it as a challenge. The king saw the fourth man in the furnace, like the Son of God.

God is the God of fire (Elijah on Mount Carmel, the tongues of fire at Pentecost, the burning bush, Mount Sinai). His Word is compared to fire. The best way to fight fire (challenge) is with fire (God's Word; God's presence).

We need a quiet time, a time alone. Not in the house, where we fight the battle but find a place in nature. Meditate and see the world differently, a place to receive.

Whatever difficulty we are facing is to take us to another level. Allow God to do His work; don't help Him out by having an alternative. If Daniel had had an alternative, they wouldn't have known which was the true God.

There are many gods – unfaithfulness, unkindness, doubt, fear. These are evil angels working against God. They know you are at Prayer Mountain, and they are at work. They are going about looking for people for their kingdom. So we have to watch and pray. They see people want to be faithful and are looking for a chink of unfaithfulness to enter through. They enter through doubt and unfaithfulness etc.

Jesus said, "let this cup pass," but then the angel corrected Him, and he saw that it had to be God's will, not His; the angels are ready to help us too.

No-one is above mistakes; immediately repent, then there is no record of wrong. There is no record for anyone who realises their mistakes immediately. How to recognise it immediately is through awareness through the Word of God. Your life, therefore, depends on knowing the Bible. It is a guide for everything you need. Make God's Word the standard for your life.

The only way to be effective for God is to stay focused. You have to chart your course alone. God's plan for every one of us is between God and that person. Righteousness is a gift from God. Everyone has it; you just need to be aware of it (like a pen in your pocket). Everything God wants you to be is within you. To make use of it is by faith. There is nothing like failure and doubt in His mind, and we are made to be like Him.

When facing crises (which are part of life), look deep enough to see the cause. When the decree was published, Daniel went to his upper room to pray. He would have been praying for the decree to be changed. If this prayer had been answered, he wouldn't have gone into the lion's den. Compare the glory to God between the lion's den and if this prayer had been answered!

If God plans to take you to where you have never been, and you are praying to go where you have been before, you can't change God's plan. Daniel couldn't pray about the lion's den because he had never been there before. When Daniel was sentenced, he stood firm and didn't change his belief or trust even though his prayer had not been answered. It is better not to be specific in prayer.

When you read about God's Generals, they prayed for God's will to be done, and they praised God; Paul and Silas praised God; they were not asking God to remove the chains. Today when we ask God for too many specific things, we get disappointed. Allow the Holy Spirit to make the requests; He is the intercessor. Jesus prayed for the will of God to be done instead of praying to let the cup pass.

Experience is the best teacher. Every minister has his own habit of approaching God."

A HOLY PLACE

The Prayer Mountain is a physical place, but the concept reaches beyond; it is about a holy heart, a pure heart. It is, therefore, more than a physical site; it is a Holy Place,

Another holy place at The SCOAN, is the altar area in the church auditorium. In the much earlier days, the church members rushed to pray there as soon as the service was closed. That was the time of the round altar.

Prophet T.B. Joshua Prays at the Altar at The SCOAN in 2019

By the time The SCOAN was becoming a more prominent place of pilgrimage, day and night, there would be men and women (in separate areas) kneeling reverently or lying face down, with their Bibles at their sides, in front of the altar. Why? They were preparing for the Sunday service, making their hearts ready to receive.

Following the development of the newer altar, there would be the Living Water Services, where water that had been anointed in Jesus' name would be fed to taps in the upper part of the altar area. Before climbing the stairs to collect this water, one would lie prostrate upon the main altar area. The healings and deliverances from this were many and varied.

Word was going around outside the church and among the visitors, 'We are going to pray on the SCOAN altar'. Queuing patiently in a long line (sometimes stretching outside the church and down the busy road), the people waited for their turn.

At one 'Living Water' service, held on Monday 3 February 2020, a 12-year-old girl saw a heavenly vision as she poured some of the

water on her eyes at The SCOAN altar,

"There is a Man there; He is tall! He is wearing a white garment," she exclaimed. "He said, 'Repent; I am coming soon. Bring people to My church; bring more souls.'"

Throughout this period, her eyes remained closed as she proclaimed, "His face is shining" and "the light is too bright".

Suddenly, the young girl crumpled to the floor and appeared to 'awaken' from the trance. Bemused at the attention surrounding her, she emotionally recounted what she had just witnessed.

"On His head was a big crown, and He was sitting on a throne," she observed, adding that she saw smoke surrounding the Heavenly scene.

The young girl was shocked that no one else saw what she had seen so vividly.

Girl Experiences a Heavenly Vision on the SCOAN Altar

"People are going on the wrong track; we should bring them back to the church," she pleaded.

"There is no excuse for being surprised by the uncertainty of coming events," T.B. Joshua stated when posting a video of this encounter on the internet later that week, "The uncertainty of the hour of Christ's return calls for vigilance and watchfulness. Let us not wait for another sign from Heaven to convince us of the paramount importance of making the most out of life today because only today is our own; tomorrow is not."[48]

This vision is somewhat reminiscent of some occurrences many years earlier in the Church of St Mary's in Everton in Bedfordshire, England. John Wesley records in his journal an interview with a 15-year-old girl called Alice, who fell into such a trance,

---

48 *"Jesus Is Coming Soon!" - Little Girl's Shocking Vision From Heaven*, TB Joshua Ministries Facebook Post, 6 Feb 2020

I found her sitting on a stool and leaning against the wall, with her eyes open and fixed upward. I made a motion as if going to strike, but they continued immovable. Her face showed an unspeakable mixture of reverence and love, while silent tears stole down her cheeks. Her lips were a little open, and sometimes moved; but not enough to cause any sound.

I do not know whether I ever saw a human face look so beautiful; sometimes it was covered with a smile, as from joy, mixing with love and reverence; but the tears fell still though not so fast. Her pulse was quite regular. In about half an hour I observed her countenance change into the form of fear, pity, and distress; then she burst into a flood of tears and cried out, 'Dear Lord; they will be damned! They will all be damned!' But in about five minutes her smiles returned, and only love and joy appeared in her face.

About half an hour after six, I observed distress take place again; and soon after she wept bitterly and cried out, 'Dear Lord, they will go to hell! The world will go to hell!' Soon after, she said, 'Cry aloud! Spare not!' And in a few moments her look was composed again and spoke a mixture of reverence, joy, and love. Then she said aloud, 'Give God the glory.' About seven her senses returned. I asked, 'Where have you been?'-- 'I have been with my Saviour.' 'In heaven, or on earth?'-- 'I cannot tell; but I was in glory.' 'Why then did you cry?'-- 'Not for myself, but for the world; for I saw they were on the brink of hell.' 'Whom did you desire to give the glory to God?'-- 'Ministers that cry aloud to the world; else they will be proud; and then God will leave them, and they will lose their own souls.'[49]

A PROPHET IN OUR TIME

It was January 2002, and the service at The SCOAN was drawing to a close. Prophet T.B. Joshua walked back and forth along a small raised balcony at the back of the auditorium, the place where he usually made the announcements about upcoming prayer vigils

---

49   Wesley, J. (1827), *The Journal of the Rev. John Wesley, Volume 2*. J. Kershaw. Entry for 6 Aug 1759, p. 454

or other meetings. But this time, there was a particularly sombre atmosphere, as quietly and unemotionally, he was warning people they should go straight home. He specifically mentioned the district of Ikeja and referred back to a previous prophecy that had warned of explosions. As a fairly recent visitor, Gary found it difficult to interpret what was happening, but the people got the message and dispersed quietly and quickly.

Then, about two or three hours later, we heard the bang and saw the flash of light in the distance. We later learned that there had been a massive explosion at a military facility in the Ikeja area of Lagos, with many killed and injured. The next morning, we saw the church compound full of those who had fled the areas close to the explosion, who had come to the church for refuge during the night. The church workers comforted them, and T.B. Joshua provided food, clothing and financial support.

Here was evidence that indeed there was a prophet in our midst.

Ghanaian Presidential Elections

"Mama Fiona, sisters," I heard breathless steps running and then the door to the office where I and others were busy answering emails was flung open, "He has won, he is going to be the President, and the prophecy has been fulfilled!"

We stood up, rejoicing, "Emmanuel, God with us! God has done it."

What was happening? A prophetic word given by T.B. Joshua was being fulfilled, and a President of a Nation was going to be inaugurated.

Later, on 11 January 2009, there would be a Sunday service attended personally by President Atta Mills just four days after his inauguration as the President of Ghana. Here, he would publicly thank God for the privilege of being in the position he now held and honour T.B. Joshua as both a friend and mentor and a prophet of God Almighty. Here is an extract of what we witnessed him saying on that day,

"When I told him [Prophet T.B. Joshua] that our elections

would be on December 7th and that there was a possibility that the results will be announced on the 8th, 9th or 10th of December, he looked at me for some time, smiled and said: "I don't see it that way; I can see three different elec-

President Atta Mills of Ghana at The SCOAN on 11 Jan 2009

tions ahead of you... and that the results are going to be declared in January." I was asking myself, if there is a runoff and the runoff is usually on the 28th of December, give ourselves two days for the electoral commissioner to come up with the result - how is it possible that we will run into January? Well, I kept these words at the back of my mind. We had the elections alright on December 7th. There was a runoff on December 28th, and then we had a third election in one constituency, and the results were announced in January."[50]

Later that year, we would join T.B. Joshua on a visit to Ghana, where we would meet President Atta Mills personally and hear from his own lips his testimony of the significance of that prophecy and of the encouragement and counsel he had received from the prophet.

A 'GREAT STAR'

On Sunday 4 January 2009, Prophet T.B. Joshua revealed a prophetic message concerning a great star who would go on a journey of no return,

> I'm seeing a great star about whom the world is shouting: 'Hey, hey, hey!' In his own area, he is famous, he is known everywhere. Great, too great! Because I see something will begin to happen to that star, which may likely end him to pack his load and go to the journey of no return. But I don't know when that journey will be.

There was to be another time, on 12 June 2009, when the prophetic

50   *Address by President Atta Mills of Ghana*. SCOAN Sunday Service, 11 Jan 2009

warning was given more directly. The man of God had said Michael Jackson needed to come to The SCOAN for deliverance. He knew all was not well and specifically conveyed this message via Tee-Mac, a celebrated local musician who was a friend of the Jackson family.[51]

Then on Thursday, 25 June 2009, international music icon and the most famous pop star of modern times, Michael Jackson, unexpectedly died following a cardiac arrest in Los Angeles, California. What a day when we saw the news, stunned as coverage of the death was played many times on all the major networks. This gifted musician had crossed the boundaries to appeal across the races, colours and creeds. Moved, we watched the footage and wondered!

The following Sunday was when Tee-Mac publicly explained during the SCOAN service his pain upon hearing about the death, and how he wished he could have made more effort to convince the star to visit The SCOAN following the personal message given to him by Prophet T.B. Joshua.

Later that year, a Jackson family member came to The SCOAN to witness the service and meet T.B. Joshua privately. This all happened during one of our times of living at The SCOAN, and we admired the low key sensitive way this visit was handled.

Truly a 'great star' had gone on a 'journey of no return'.

THE WEEPING PROPHET

"I hurt with the hurt of my people. I mourn and am overcome with grief." (Jeremiah 8:21, NLT)

At the beginning of September 2019 in South Africa, there was a spate of attacks by mobs on non-nationals, many of whom were Nigerian. Unrest was increasing, and retaliation and an escalation of violence were looking inevitable.

---

51 *Death In The House: Michael Jackson's Brother Runs to TB Joshua,* The Nigerian Voice, 2 Aug 2009

For the Sunday service in The SCOAN on 8 September, Prophet T.B. Joshua did not preach. Indeed he did not participate in the service except to stand in line hand in hand with The SCOAN choir on the stage as they sang a song he had written entitled Africa Unite! He was visibly moved and shed tears during the song,

> *Africa unite*
> *[Africa remember where we are coming from]*
> *Africa unite*
> *[Africa let us unite]*
> *We need each other*
> *We need one another to grow*
> *Africa unite*
> *The South cannot do it alone*
> *The West cannot go it alone*
> *The East cannot do it alone*
> *The North cannot go it alone*
> *We need each other*
> *We need one another to grow*
> *Africa unite*

During the following two weeks, The SCOAN received about 200 Nigerian 'returnees' at the church to hear their testimonies and to give them some tangible support in the form of cash donations totalling 15 million naira. The returnees' stories explained the impact of the song and Prophet T.B. Joshua's tears,

> "Before that song of Prophet T.B. Joshua, there was anger within the Nigerian community. We were sending messages back to Nigeria, sharing horrible videos and calling on our people to revenge the attacks. But after that song, I was delivered from that anger, malice, grievances. It was a self-deliverance. I realised our enemy is not the physical appearance but a person

without flesh or blood – spirit-beings."
(Mr Stanley, Nigerian returnee)[52]

"The tears that Prophet T.B. Joshua shed last Sunday during the live Sunday Service broadcast saved many lives."
(Mr Nwaocha, Nigerian returnee)[53]

"It was the tears of the man of God that made the police rally round us in saving us from the attackers. We must show love to one another."
(Mr Ogbonna, Nigerian returnee)[54]

THE PANDEMIC ERA

The 'Faith Resort Ground', or 'Prayer Mountain', was a project taking many years to develop. The swampy 'bush' would be painstakingly drained by labourers often working in simple boats by hand to remove the reeds. Over time this created an expanse of water. With its small islands, this lake became a haven for birds, and sunset would see the air filled with them. Small monkeys, peacocks and gentle antelopes, as well as ornamental cocks, were also to be seen.

The Prayer Mountain in Early 2021

Slowly the large Prayer Garden area would emerge with new trees chosen to provide shade for the praying pilgrims. Special drainage channels were created so the tropical rains could quickly disperse, and finally, the Prayer Walkway around the lake was constructed, being completed during 2020.

Outside the Prayer Mountain, the traffic roared, and busy megacity

---

52   *South Africa returnees narrate ordeals,* P.M. News (Nigeria), 20 Sep 2019
53   *South African returnees get financial aid, succour from SCOAN,* Nigerian Tribune, 15 Sep 2019
54   Ibid.

life continued, but inside the high walls, an oasis of nature and peace had emerged.

One memory that stands out was the significant crossover between 2019 and 2020 (when the virus that caused the COVID-19 pandemic was already at work in China). The man of God chose to spend that time at the Lagos Prayer Mountain with about 300 visitors rather than appearing live on Emmanuel TV as an 'influencer' as the New Year began. Already the 'Prayer Walkway' was nearly completed, and in the heat of the day, 'to sweat the flesh', as T.B. Joshua encouraged us, we walked and uttered the prayer points,

> *Every spirit of offence, you are not welcome here! Get out of my life!*
> *Every spirit of hatred, you are not welcome here! Get out of my life!*
> *Every spirit of immorality, you are not welcome here! Get out of my life!*
> *Every spirit of unfaithfulness, you are not welcome here! Get out of my life!*
> *Every pain of the past, you are not welcome here! Get out of my life!*

> *Thank You, Holy Spirit of love, for forgiving my hatred*
> *Thank You, Holy Spirit of faith, for forgiving my doubt*
> *Thank You, Holy Spirit of hope, for forgiving my self-pity*
> *Thank You, Holy Spirit of humility, for forgiving my pride*
> *Thank You, Holy Spirit of peace, for forgiving my anger*
> *Thank You, Holy Spirit of patience, for forgiving my grumbling*
> *Thank You, Holy Spirit of goodness, for forgiving my evil deeds*

As a prophet, a communicator between the visible and the invisible, he prophesied amongst many other accurate prophecies, the year of fear, saying, "You people are not concerned, but I am very concerned." It happened as foretold. The year of fear that would affect every nation was about to break upon us. This would change what we formerly regarded as ordinary life from the inside out. Every nation would be affected as the plague of fear gripped all, especially the developed countries with their considerably older demographic and concern about overwhelmed health systems. Churches everywhere closed their doors and prepared to minister 'online'.

"I knew a time like this would come," said the man of God, referring to the shuttering of churches. Indeed the herculean efforts over the years to prepare the Prayer Mountain area as a suitable place for many hundreds of people with abundant space, fresh air and the inspiration of nature were now rewarded. Emmanuel TV Partners and church members were the first beneficiaries of this blessed space.

As time passed, T.B. Joshua would be seen ministering to Emmanuel TV Partners in prayer at the Prayer Mountain. Walking amongst the trees in the garden, a sylvan setting, he took his time, moving amongst the people who sat arranged in an orderly socially-distanced manner waiting for that touch from Jesus. Faithful Emma-

nuel TV friends and partners had waited for such a long time to receive that anointed touch. Anointed it was indeed; long term chronic conditions such as poor vision, limited mobility and arthritis would flee away as their father in the Lord moved amongst the trees, and the power of God was present to heal.

T.B. Joshua Prays for Emmanuel TV Partners in the Prayer Garden

OUR SPIRITUAL LIFE

Prophet T.B. Joshua often said that,

"The first place you are to prosper is in your spiritual life."

Without that foundation, any other form of prosperity will not stand the test of time or could end up being a destructive force rather than a blessing.

But how do we build our spiritual life? The following sermon helps shed light on this.

OUR SPIRITUAL LIFE

T.B. Joshua, The SCOAN Sunday Service, 7 February 2010

Many of us are traditional Christians who are used to one method of praying or the other. It is not our body that prays, but the one inside us (who we cannot see) that prays. There are two natures in one person; the one we can see is the human nature. It is not only when you open your lips that you are praying. You can be praying and holding discussions with friends, or you can be praying and eating at the same time.

This should be the normal life of a Christian, i.e. your life should be a life of prayer. You need to meditate in the name of Jesus Christ always, saying, *"Lord Jesus, have mercy on me; let Your mercy speak for me; let Your favour speak for me today"*. But how many Christians do this? You only pray when you are in need.

Our problem is that we are too worldly and what we are looking for in the world, which is consuming all our quality time, effort and energy, we are not getting it. This is the most disappointing thing. Why then can't we give more time for our spiritual life and get connected and see what will happen?

The proceeds of your being born again, your being a believer, are enough to tell the world who you are instead of you introducing yourself. Today, you are the one begging people to let you pray for them, instead of them begging you for prayer after recognising Jesus in you.

You need Jesus always, not only at a certain time. You know you need Jesus, but you don't know how much you need Him. You need Him to put on your spectacles, you need Him to open your lips, you need Him to close your mouth, you need Him to look behind or in front, but you believe you only need Jesus when there is trouble or difficulty. That is why satan keeps using this opportunity; he knows the time you call Him, the time you need Him. Those times you are not connected, he gets at you, he strikes.

When you begin to think you can do certain things on your own, you get it wrong. You must be dependent on Him for everything. Paul the Apostle says, *"I can do all things through Christ who strengthens me"* (Philippians 4:13), but for you, it is not all things that you do through Christ today. You do not look through Christ; you do not smile through Christ; you do not rise, sit or eat through Christ.

We need to start building our spiritual life afresh. When you meditate on Jesus all the time, you will not have time for rubbish; you will not go where Jesus is not welcome. You should always be in an attitude of prayer all the time and not wait until I say, "Rise up for prayer". The first place we are to prosper is in our spiritual life

The greatest war we have is in our heart. Hardship and disappointment will first happen in our hearts, but when we are in an attitude of prayer, all of these negative thoughts will disappear.

The situation of a Christian is meant for the glory of God, like what happened to Paul,

"Concerning this thing, I pleaded with the Lord three times that it might depart from me. And He said to me, 'My grace is sufficient for you, for My strength is made perfect in weakness.'" (2 Corinthians 12:8-9)

When God is aware of your situation, He will manifest His strength in your weakness. You can go on and on with the problem until He decides to remove it or not to remove it. And if He decides not to remove it, you can still live the rest of your life peacefully because we never learnt that it was the thorn that killed Paul.

A Christian lives a life that comes from Christ, and when your life comes from Christ, anything about it, Christ is aware, unless you don't derive your inner resources from Him. When God is aware of your situation, your situation is under control. Your situation is under control when it is meant to keep you for a new level in life, when it is meant to strengthen your desire for God, when it makes you pray the more and fast the more, and when the situation is meant to preserve you for redemption.

Still, in verse 9, Paul said, *"Therefore, I take pleasure in infirmity"*, meaning that his infirmity was different from others. Others' are meant to destroy them, meant to kill them, but yours is meant to preserve you, to keep you for a new level and to prepare you for the challenges ahead. If that is your situation, then why murmur, why complain, why doubt, why fear? It is an opportunity for you to honour God before men.

But today, when you are having a little trouble, without being told, people can see it from your appearance. The sympathy of human beings cannot solve your problem; it will rather make it worse. So stay true to God. In good or hard times, stay true to God.

You are a chosen generation. When you do not know who you are, you begin to compare yourself with others. Take your situation back from satan by seeing it as a blessing and an opportunity to honour God before men.

A MAN OF THE PEOPLE

"*To the weak I became as weak, that I might win the weak. I have become all things to all men, that I might by all means save some.*" (1 Corinthians 9:22)

Hebrews 1 verse 9 speaks of Jesus Christ, quoting one of the Psalms,

"You have loved righteousness and hated lawlessness; therefore God, Your God, has anointed You with the oil of gladness more than Your companions."

In his dealings with humanity at large, another picture of T.B. Joshua emerges, a joy-filled one, which sees him relating to every man, woman and child at their level. He demonstrates being 'all things to all men', a man of God and a man of the people.

Perhaps nowhere was this more evident than in dealing with people responding to a prophetic word or asking questions in the live church service. Let us join this scene one day.

A little boy sits somewhat nervously by his mother, who, as T.B. Joshua is walking by, starts to behave strangely due to the effect of evil spirits in her life. The mother is trying to explain that the little boy is the one with the problem (anger), but T.B. Joshua is having nothing of it. Whilst the mother is under the influence of the Holy Spirit, he is both praying for her and at the same time making the little child feel at ease.

All caught on camera, and for viewers worldwide to see, he first asks him what is in his pockets and then takes his miniature suit jacket and tries to put it on himself. The little one's face lights up, and a ripple of laughter spreads across his face. You can see by the body language he relaxes, 'So this big adult in this big place is a funny man. I like this man.' The scene ends with him taking T.B. Joshua by the hand happily; together, they walk towards his mother, who has now finished her deliverance. He then says to the mother, "He is a good boy, later I will see you both".

> "In a situation where there are tension and pressure, laughing becomes a great relief."

'Religious spirits' would be quivering as T.B. Joshua would demonstrate humour and laughter to expose them.

One couple came for prayer, with the husband complaining that the wife would consult the Bible before taking any action, including marital intimacy issues. Sounding serious and probing deeper, he questioned the exasperated husband whose stories revealed a malignant religious spirit behind his wife's actions. Tackling the subject with his gentle humour exposed the superstitious religious spirit that, without deliverance, could lead to mental illness. The example spoke as a living parable to the church and wider audience.

Giving her the Bible, he asked her to act out how she consulted it by opening at random and deciding which market stall she would visit to buy yam (a local vegetable). As the examples grew ever more ridiculous, the church's laughter proved an apt way of exposing the malign force at work. Following deliverance, the couple came to share their testimony. A marriage restored and a bright future ahead.

Anything can happen at any time at a SCOAN service. One minute the congregation, often gorgeously dressed in bright cotton local attire, would be falling about laughing; another minute, there would be a prophecy, "Someone here has a weapon. Come out. God will deliver you." A man would then come to the front, drawn by the influence of the Holy Spirit, and, as he raised his trousers, a foot-long knife could be spotted, tied around his calf.

Accessible yet Untouchable

It was the middle of the church service, and outside, sounds of gunshots fill the air! There were armed robbers in the street, threat-

ening to cause havoc with a loaded gun. In the crowded streets, thronging with people, there was opportunity to cause carnage quickly.

Calmly T.B. Joshua walked out, approached the robbers in the midst of the crowd, demanded the gun, and then carried the weapon into the church and continued his preaching.

T.B. Joshua Displays the Gun Retrieved from Armed Robbers

On another occasion, a man carrying acid jumped on the car as T.B. Joshua was about to get in it to return to the Prayer Mountain from the church. The man of God spoke a word of authority, and the man 'froze' and was unable to discharge his evil deed.

Walking amid crowds of people in the church, Prophet T.B. Joshua would comment that, walking with God, he was 'accessible but untouchable'.

These incidents were not confined to the church premises or even Nigeria.

"Quick, Stop him; where is he going?" The burly man headed straight across the prayer area, running purposely towards T.B. Joshua, intending to knock him to the ground.

"What is happening?" As he gets very close, it is as though he encounters a solid wall, and he falls to the ground, unable to rise.

This was not in Lagos but thousands of miles away in Singapore.

We read about a similar phenomenon in some detail in the journals of the founders of Methodism, John and Charles Wesley, who were occasionally set upon by violent mobs during their open-air preaching endeavours. It was not uncommon for mob leaders to change sides and start to protect them, as they came under the power of the word spoken in love and faith. One prominent thug called Munchin had this experience, and, having set out to kill John Wesley, he ended up protecting him from the rest of the mob. Charles Wesley wrote of him,

> Munchin, the former captain of the mob, has been constantly under the Word since he rescued my brother. I asked him what he thought of him. "Think of him!" said he: "That he is a man of God, and God was on his side when so many of us could not kill one man.[55]

Returning to the present, a group of militants came to The SCOAN because they were tired of violence and the relentless desire for bloodshed and wanted deliverance.[56] They saw in T.B. Joshua a man they could approach. As he has said, "No one is too bad, and no one is too good to receive salvation".

DANCING AND CELEBRATIONS

What was the camera showing? A below-knee shot of twirling feet tap-tapping to a vigorous beat. Who was the person? Now we could see; there was T.B. Joshua dancing, as all around the joyful cacophony of instruments, African drums and voices swirled. It was the live Sunday service with everyone enjoying the opportunity to praise God with a bit of genuine West African rhythm, none more so than the pastor.

T.B. Joshua Dances During a Time of Praise

55   Jackson, T. (Ed.) (1849). *The Journal of the Rev. Charles Wesley*. Entry for 25 Oct 1743
56   *Nigerian Militants Surrender In Church!* TB Joshua Ministries Facebook Post, 26 Jun 2019

The New Year celebrations saw this love of dancing raised to a different level. First, there was food for the visitors who had come for a week's spiritual retreat and all the church workers. After tasting the delicious spread of local and international food, the dancing competitions would begin. First, the different nations took the floor, and then the church's work departments.

There would be official comperes, who would announce the results with great seriousness. Sometimes, T.B. Joshua would send a message to the evangelists, and before we knew it, everyone would find themselves live on Emmanuel TV. The phones would begin popping as Text and Whatsapp messages would flood in, especially from Southern African countries, saying 'I am watching you; nice dancing; wish I was there!'

Boxing in the Spirit

There were few things the stalwart local church members, especially the muscular Nigerian men, would enjoy more than the power encounters that the Holy Spirit occasionally permitted T.B. Joshua to have with well-known boxers or wrestlers.

Although there was a great deal of laughter from those watching, these encounters helped build faith and shame the devil.

There was the boxer who came for deliverance, where T.B. Joshua proclaimed, "I am going to box you in the spirit". The boxer, a tall Nigerian with bulging biceps, squares up automatically. Although he wanted deliverance, surely this moderately sized non-boxer was not going to get him down. What about his reputation?

But this is a boxing match not from the flesh but the spirit. With no physical touching, as T.B. Joshua boxes the air in his direction, he falls to the ground once, twice, thrice. At the end of Round 3, he bows his head to the ground. T.B. Joshua throws out a commanding wave in his direction, and the man crumples to the floor again, finally delivered.

After that, with a glint in his eye, some advice to the man about his boxing. "If it is your profession as a sportsman, continue your boxing but do not hate your opponent."

Cheers and hands thrown in the air greeted this encounter from the watching church members, and they went home to tell their neighbours all about it.

Another time, an elderly refined white South African lady admitted she was fearful of being mugged. T.B. Joshua took her handbag, gave it back to her and told others from her South African group to try and snatch the bag. She raised her handbag as they came near, even

two at a time, and proclaimed, "In the name of Jesus, you will not carry my bag." One by one, they failed and ended up lying on the floor, unable to comprehend. Was this really happening to strong, competent men? What was this power?

A Crowded Church Service at The SCOAN

On other occasions, T.B. Joshua would touch the microphone and then point it towards a person manifesting evil spirits who would fall over. He was demonstrating the anointing of God through inanimate objects.

As time would pass and the Anointing Water would be distributed widely, there would be testimonies such as holding the Anointing Water in front of armed robbers and the criminals running away.

THE SUNDAY SCHOOL

As T.B. Joshua visited the Sunday School classes and passed by them (often with showers of sweets), there were always shouts and squeals of joy. Children called him Papa and wanted to be with him. Children's birthdays were celebrated with a cake, and he would often cut the cake.

Then there were the performances in front of the church by the children. The camera team always recorded the children's rehearsed events with as much seriousness as they would give to the Sunday service. As Emmanuel TV grew, the best of these might appear in the schedule.

What an exciting time; it is the Sunday School's opportunity to shine.

T.B. Joshua Celebrates a Sunday School Birthday in 2002

They have prepared a special performance and, giggling, they try to remember their lines. The mothers are working on their costumes and keeping order. Our groups of visitors loved the little ones' live performances, and this time was no exception.

Here comes a young boy and with him a group of children who line up in a row. The little boy's fake moustache is a bit loose, but his aplomb is considerable. Walking up to the line of children, he begins to pray, "You spirit of naughtiness and dull brain, out of this body! I command you to leave in Jesus' name!" Turning to the audience, once his whole row of 'patients' are on the floor, he begins to lead with some of T.B. Joshua's prayer points, imperiously calling for the camera so he can pray for the viewers.

The visitors do not escape his eagle eye, and although not in our midst, we know that elsewhere in the building, T.B. Joshua, with his effervescent sense of humour, is loving the imitation of himself.

Later on, the best preachers from amongst the children would join the performance to preach. Then there was perhaps our favourite example: A themed discussion by the ten-year-olds on a sober theological theme, perhaps the nature of prayer or the role of the Holy Spirit. This was unashamedly a gentle, humorous way to explain and demonstrate eternal truths and how well it succeeded!

It is prayer time in the live service, and a small boy with a mischievous face is sitting with his mother. He is bold and laughs aloud when he sees T.B. Joshua in the flesh. This child has come prepared, and he asks for the microphone, reducing T.B. Joshua to shouts of laughter. He asks the boy, "Do you want to preach?"

A Small Boy Imitates T.B. Joshua Preaching in 2011

The boy has memorised a sequence from Emmanuel TV, quoting complex scriptures and also teaching points, such as, "Knowledge means to explain the unfolding and correlation of Gospel facts," and, "Prophecy is not necessarily predicting events but preaching and teaching the Word with power!"

This encounter, as well as giving great joy to the child and the watching church, was a spontaneous opportunity for the pastor to encourage parents to observe the scriptural injunction to 'Train up your children in the way of the Lord'. This particular boy grew and flourished and was often seen with his mother at The SCOAN in holiday times.

And what was the result of such an encounter? Did it end there? Was it just a bit of light-hearted fun during the service? The clip was watched on YouTube many times over and in many countries. In Pakistan, at Emmanuel School, it was considerably appreciated by the teachers and children.

MENTORING

People of all ages from many nations would ask to stay for a while at The SCOAN to be mentored by T.B. Joshua. It was and is a 'Bible School of the Holy Spirit' where money is not required in any way. He was also clear about the absolute necessity to maintain any impartation received by good character and consistently living by the Word of God.

As well as the evangelists, this mentoring has taken many forms, such as developing the church's youth, who would learn valuable skills from working in different departments. This experience would stand them in good stead for their future careers.

Emmanuel TV, in particular, has benefitted from this in-house training. As the website explains,

> We at Emmanuel TV believe in skill development. Jesus Christ took time to develop His disciples' skills. All of our production team, including the cameramen, editors, directors, graphic designers, artists, presenters, sound engineers, etc., are all in-house evangelists who have developed their skills through working at The SCOAN and with Emmanuel TV.

Some prominent people would come to the church to see the man of God in his office to seek the wisdom of a recognised prophet. These would include businessmen and women, academics, government officials and humanitarians, as well as pastors. Some like Nicodemus visiting Jesus would come unobtrusively, by night.

T.B. Joshua always encouraged people to do 'better than their best' whether their skills lie in academia, law, medicine, business, sport, the arts or ministry.

WORKS OF CHARITY

T.B. Joshua could relate personally to the poor, and throughout his life, he devoted himself to giving generously to help them. Here is an extract of a newspaper interview with him which explains some background:

What informed your passion for the needy?

T.B. Joshua Visiting the Needy in 2007

'The Bible says, "Watch and pray..." – it means you need to look around before you pray. If there are people who need your help, do whatever you can to give them relief: love them. After this, pray – and your prayers would be answered. I know what it is to be in need. I have once been in this situation, asking for help. I know perfectly well what it means to be in need. I have tasted poverty, humiliation. I suffered dejection, neglect and what have you. But today, I am a product of grace. I do not blame anyone for being poor; I should not blame anyone for being humiliated. The fast runner does not always win the race.'[57]

T.B. Joshua made no secret of his love for his country. As part of the many local charity projects and scholarship schemes, he would often help those who had tried to reach a 'better life' in Europe, having been duped by unscrupulous people-smugglers. This 'better life' frequently saw them locked in Libyan prisons or working as 'modern slaves'. There would be appeals for help to T.B. Joshua, and the Nigerian Government would be involved in repatriation.

Dressed in regulation tracksuits, the Libya deportees would come to The SCOAN and receive food, medical care and spiritual nour-

ishment before receiving financial assistance and bags of rice to help them return to their birthplaces. First, they would tell their harrowing stories in front of a packed church and many more watching on Emmanuel TV, warning others not to fall for the lies promising an easy route to 'greener pastures'.

Nigerians Deported from Libya Receive Support at The SCOAN in 2017

HAITI

"Baba and Mama, are you sitting down? We have a big assignment." T.B. Joshua had called in the middle of the night, saying the five of us in the US should spearhead a response to the catastrophic Haiti earthquake of January 2010, with a medical clinic. In Colorado, we had been setting up a small office for Emmanuel TV when that call came in the early morning from one of the team. Following that instruction to go, ten days later, the US team, with support from the UK, had chartered a cargo plane, filled it with medical supplies and assembled a project team. That in itself was a miracle.

Fiona describes her feelings at the time,

They were a mixture of 'how amazing' and 'how terrifying' all at once. The political situation was uncertain. We were all expected to sleep directly on the ground on rocks (as it happened), living out of small rucksacks. Now, the fuel supply in Haiti was uncertain. The smallest I had been on, our tiny plane had to stop to pick up fuel in Nassau. But as I sat on the 9-seater, these were the prevailing thoughts in my mind, 'I am at peace with everybody; I am going to serve the poor; God is with us, and we are under the direction of a true prophet, so whatever happens, it is well.'

Gary had stayed behind in Florida for a few days to sort out the cargo plane, where he experienced his share of challenges and miracles. The first plane was grounded, but then a second charter company was identified, and a new plane prepared and loaded, all within 24 hours. After he arrived with the cargo plane and supplies in Haiti

and met up with Fiona and other team members, the next miracle was getting the goods down to the earthquake zone. We travelled on officially impassable roads the whole length of the island and then asked the Mayor of Arcahaie for a piece of land to camp in and use as a clinic.

Once we were there, there was no problem finding needy people. All

Gary and Fiona on Local Transport in Haiti

the pregnant women wanted to see a Doctor, and all the children needed treatment from bad water. The people were terrified following the earthquake and sleeping outside.

Haiti (that part) was extremely poor, and the local market looked as if it was from 300 years ago, the goods arriving on donkeys.

A clear message from T.B. Joshua to the assembled team was to live more like the locals and, by inference, avoid the pitfalls of staying in comfortable hotels far removed from the actual way of life of those we were trying to assist. How right was the man of God; the locals instantly saw the difference.

Some Food Provisions at the Emmanuel TV Medical Clinic in Arcahaie

A big lesson from the experiences in Haiti was that moving forward involves discomfort. In Haiti, the discomfort was physical - relentless heat, no proper toilet, cooking simple meals for the team on a charcoal fire, sleeping on a layer of cardboard, showering with half a bucket of water for weeks on end - but It was amazing and life-changing! Other situations for moving forward might involve different challenges, perhaps mental or emotional rather than physical.

THE MAN AND THE MESSAGE

The simple call from T.B. Joshua while we were 'sitting comfortably' in Colorado had led to the establishment of a long term medical clinic in Haiti, with a string of miracles and lives changed for the better along the way. How was it that this message had carried with it the power of fulfilment and had shown ample evidence of being backed up by God? For this, we need to understand something more about this man of the people.

T.B. Joshua was a man who is inseparable from his message. He said essentially the same things when he stood to speak in a Sunday service or spoke to you one to one. Whether it was prepared or unprepared, he spoke out of what he was meditating about.

If you wanted to find out how he was thinking or whether he had a message specifically for you, most of the time, you only had to listen carefully to what he said publicly. Nothing was hidden. The secret of his ministry was an open secret.

An early message we heard preached was titled, "Talk what you believe". For T.B. Joshua, this was not a slogan but a simple description of how he communicated You can find out what you actually believe (as opposed to what you think you believe) by observing your daily behaviour and listening to your everyday conversation. For many of us, this is often different from what we confess to believe. But the two must come together if we are going to have any real impact for good.

A good example is our approach to prayer. To caricature how we too often go about it, it goes like this: We prepare ourselves, we travel to the meeting, and then we pray out loud, believing that (provided we pray 'in faith') God hears our prayer. But T.B. Joshua makes a clear distinction between praying prayers and saying words, explaining that we must be in an attitude of prayer at all times. He explains that the prayer that sees healing, deliverance and miracles in his ministry is not the one he speaks out loud, but the prayer he is continually offering in his heart. For the prayer for all, known as 'mass prayer', the spoken word of authority adds to the constant prayer of the heart and brings results, "Be Healed! Be delivered!"

God hears the prayer of the heart, not just the prayer of the voice. And if your heart is not free from worry or offence, for example, then however impressive the words of prayer that you might speak, you will hear yourself, and those around will hear you, but God will not hear you.

It is the same with our wanting to follow Jesus. It is one thing to say we want to follow Jesus, but another thing to mean it with our whole heart. Without that commitment from the heart, we will not stand the test of time. As the man of God put it quite dramatically in a sermon in 2017,

I decided to follow Jesus, and I meant it with all my heart. If I didn't mean it, by now, you would be pointing to my graveyard, or you would be giving history that there used to be a church called The SCOAN.[58]

You can't fool God. Christianity is not a performance but a relationship. People may look at what we do, but Jesus sees why we do it; people may see the action, but God sees the motive behind the action.

As T.B. Joshua also put it,

"Jesus Christ never strived to look good; he simply was good."

Another way of looking at this is that it is all about love,

"Love is the real measure of true spirituality."

By observing his example and listening to his messages on love, we saw that a particular feature of love is that it concerns the here and now - the present. Acts of love are the 'natural' outcomes of a heart set free by God's love and forgiveness. To show love, you have to "stay current", you have to be alert, you have to unburden your heart. You will love yourself because God loves you, and you will love your neighbour as yourself.

EMMANUEL SCHOOL PAKISTAN

"God has people to meet you in the place of your assignment."

This word of wisdom from T.B. Joshua, reflecting upon the story of Joseph, was to be true for our travels and, in particular, for our connection with Pakistan.

During our Russian travels with the Anointing Water, we were put in contact with a pastor from Pakistan. Communicating by Skype, he indicated he had been watching the video clips (internet permitting) of Prophet T.B. Joshua and had been impressed seeing the power of God in action. We learned that his church was in a very

---

58 *Acting on the Word*, Sermon by T.B. Joshua, SCOAN Sunday Service, 14 May 2017

humble area. The direction we had received from our mentor was to go 'from country to country', so we accepted an invitation to visit to hold some healing services. In one sense, we were venturing into the unknown.

Wondering what potential challenges and adventures lay ahead, at Dubai airport we sent an email to The SCOAN to say we were shortly about to board for Pakistan. We swiftly got an email back with a message from Prophet T.B. Joshua to say he was praying for us. We knew he was, but hearing it made all the difference.

Bishop Asif Jamali, who spoke English, and his brother Rev. Khalid Jamali came to meet us from the airport. As the rented vehicle turned into the narrow medieval-style streets of Asif Town in Lahore, little did we know it would be the start of an ongoing relationship. The church members and local community would begin to know T.B. Joshua as a 'Papa' who cared about their bodies, whether they had enough to eat, as well as their spiritual lives.

Bishop Asif Jamali recounts his side of the story,

> "I had been a pastor since 1999 but I was like 'brass and jingle'. I was just empty and making noise - serving and preaching but without the power of anointing. People came to church, attended the meetings, but there was no real progress or growth. Meanwhile, I heard about T.B. Joshua from Russia and I watched videos on YouTube. And I wondered how God was using this man of God. Then in May 2011, evangelists brother Gary and sister Fiona came to Pakistan with anointed water. God worked in the lives of hundreds of people. Miracles were happening in the name of Jesus Christ. I was surprised!
>
> I kept praying that I would get to see this great man of God. One day, I suddenly received a phone call from the man of God T.B. Joshua, who talked to me and invited me to see him. Then again in November 2011, brother Gary and sister Fiona came to Pakistan, and when we went out to pray we saw many children who did not go to school."[59]

59   Private communication

During this second visit to Pakistan, we met a boy aged ten asking for prayer for a breakthrough to earn some money to help support his family. As we considered this clear example of poverty, we remembered a principle we had seen and heard in T.B. Joshua: There are two sides to the Gospel - the message of eternal salvation by faith in Christ alone and the command to love your neighbour, irrespective of their religion, culture or beliefs.

> "The demonstration of love for the needy alone is not enough to bring us to salvation, but it forms the basis for judging our level of kindness because looking the other way when your brother is in trouble is equal to rejecting Christ Himself."

Following our experience with this boy and observing how few of the women who attended the meetings had learned to read, we started discussions with Bishop Asif Jamali about the possibility of a charity school to provide high-quality free education in the local community. We began to think about how we might suggest the funding of a whole school to T.B. Joshua, while our host worked on some preliminary plans.

Meanwhile, there was the opportunity to give provisions to some widows on behalf of Emmanuel TV. The ladies from the local community in Pakistan, with their colourful clothes and loosely draped head coverings, were so grateful for the large sacks of flour they received. On behalf of Emmanuel TV, we were also able to bless some individuals with sewing machines to help generate some income.

Widows in Pakistan Receive Gifts of Flour and Sewing Machines

We sent some still pictures of this charity work to the team at The SCOAN in Lagos. To our surprise, we received a personal phone call from T.B. Joshua, encouraging us and promising to send a gift of US

$10,000 to assist this needy community further. Shortly afterwards, a follow-up call from the church Banking Department informed us that the gift had increased to US $20,000.

At that time, we had made no mention of the potential school project to T.B. Joshua or the team while waiting for Bishop Asif Jamali to prepare some practical proposals and costs. The spontane-

ous gift for unidentified 'charity work' turned out to be the exact amount needed for the school building project, which was to consist of seven classrooms built on top of Shield Of Faith Pentecostal Church. No lengthy discussions or Committee meetings - Emmanuel School was born supernaturally!

Inauguration of Emmanuel School in Pakistan on 9 March 2012

Bishop Asif Jamali picks up the story again,

> "The construction work began. There was excitement among the people of the area. The building was completed and now the school had to be named. For the inauguration ceremony on 9 March 2012, T.B. Joshua gave the name 'Emmanuel School'.
>
> Immediately after the inauguration, I traveled with brother Gary and sister Fiona to The SCOAN in Nigeria. This was my first visit. I humbly bowed before the Lord and prayed for God to send this anointing to Pakistan too. It was a blessing for me to be taken to the Prayer Mountain, where I sat in the same boat with the man of God, T.B. Joshua, and he was driving the boat. Prayers were said for me in the prayer line. And when I was about to return, I met T.B. Joshua, the man of God, and I thanked him for the school.
>
> The man of God laid his hands on my head and prayed. Three times he prayed for me and blessed me. When I left the office, it was as if a great fire of the Holy Spirit was burning inside me. I sat there and drank 10 glasses of water! When I returned to

Pakistan, the people of my church were waiting for the blessing. God changed my life and service through T.B. Joshua. Now people come in droves and are blessed. My ministry, my church and my family are blessed and fruitful. May God bless the man of God even more."

The whole school experience, what a blessing! T.B. Joshua and Emmanuel TV Partners also financed some extra land to make a playground adjoining the school and have continued to support the running of the school year after year.

PESHAWAR CHURCH BOMBING

There were many examples of giving that were 'unsung', just business as usual.

As the live service on Emmanuel TV was about to get going on 22 September 2013, we received a call from Peshawar, Pakistan. We had visited Peshawar, close to the border with Afghanistan, the previous year at the invitation of Rev. Samson of the Church of Pakistan, to take a large outdoor healing service using the Anointing Water.

The voice on the phone was trying to be calm. It was Rev. Samson.

"Mama Fiona, have you seen the news? There is a bomb attack; they are still rescuing people, many have their limbs shattered, and many have died."

Gary immediately checked the Pakistan news, and it was indeed a calamity. It had been the deadliest attack on the Christian minority in the history of Pakistan. The twin suicide bombing had taken place at All Saints Church - part of the Church Of Pakistan, whose Bishop had so warmly welcomed us the previous year.

Rev. Samson had been present at the service but was unharmed. He was now trying to coordinate some immediate relief efforts. What could we do? We managed to get a phone call through to T.B. Joshua, even though he was preparing for the service. His instant reaction was, "Can you get the money through to them safely? We want to give $10,000." He later spoke to Rev. Samson personally.

Rev. Samson was to manage some of the relief effort directly, whilst the remainder of the donation was handled by a coordinated Church of Pakistan relief programme.

Relief Effort Supported by T.B. Joshua in Peshawar

Then when we were at The SCOAN in January 2014, T.B. Joshua handed us another US $5,000 in cash to give personally to Rev. Samson to help further with the victims of the bomb blast.

EARTHQUAKE RELIEF IN ECUADOR

We were just finishing a project in the UK to source some specialist computer equipment for Emmanuel TV when we received a call from The SCOAN. An evangelist came on the line just as we were discussing 'what next in our lives'. God's timing is astounding. The evangelist said, "Hold on for the man of God." We treated these calls very seriously, and Fiona clasped her hands together, praying. A jovial voice, "How are you?" (thank God for a good connection), then it came, "You people should go to Ecuador". Then the call was over. God would lead us to the next step.

It was 21 April 2016, shortly after the major earthquake in Ecuador of 16 April 2016.

Following a short trip to The SCOAN to see the computer equipment arrive there safely, we arrived in Ecuador with just a few phone numbers as potential contacts. An Emmanuel TV team member, one of the evangelists in training, joined us from Colombia after 24 hours. Our first adventure was an overnight local bus journey to the badly affected city of Portoviejo.

A relative of one of our contacts met us to drive us around the affected areas for the day. We sat squashed together on a simple

A Visit to Portoviejo in Ecuador Following the 2016 Earthquake

bench seat and saw the driver's face change as a phone call that would change his life came in. It was from the Government, releasing a seven-figure payment due to him for many months for a Government contract.

Our driver, for that was how he was introduced, saw this as a mighty breakthrough and believed it was because he was assisting a team sent by T.B. Joshua who wanted to help his people. This man was then to tell us he was an architect. Later, we discovered he was quite a prominent architect, but he had not been not too proud to volunteer as our driver. He was subsequently to become the architect for the school rebuilding project. It was supernatural. God was involved.

It was not straightforward to identify how to get help from Emmanuel TV directly to the affected people. However, our mentor was supporting in prayer, and we received a call with a message from him that we should work closely with the Government.

We managed to secure an audience with the Governor of Esmeraldas Province. We asked if she knew of any community badly affected by the earthquake that had not yet received much help. She referred us to the indigenous village of San Salvador de los Chachis deep inside the rainforest.

The following day, sitting in a basic vehicle, we drove for many hours through simple villages. We were dressed for a smart office meeting with unsuitable footwear for the 'bush' and were utterly unprepared for what lay ahead. Leaving the rough road, we turned up a track, grimly holding on as the car bumped along. We got out of the car by the river and entered the basic canoe. Here we sat in the pouring rain for a river journey of about two hours. The canoe nearly sunk, or that is what it felt like. The long leafy branches of giant trees bent near the river, and there were eddying pools of water. We wondered a bit uneasily whether there might be crocodiles. But somewhere inside Fiona's mind, an unbelievable exhilaration was rising,

First Journey by Canoe to San Salvador de los Chachis

'Am I really in a canoe in a rainforest going to meet an indigenous tribe? How amazing is that?' I cannot remember ever being so wet before and knowing there would be no drying out for hours.

We met the Chachi community, saw the terrible conditions, learned about the school, which had been badly damaged, and then started the canoe journey home. Soon there would be a severe 'replica' aftershock, and more of the school would collapse.

San Salvador After the Earthquake

The outline of a relief project began to come together - food and hygiene aid for the Government 'displaced persons' camps and some form of support for the Chachi community. The food and hygiene aid was to be sourced in Colombia, where some churches had volunteered to help Emmanuel TV, so it was off to Bogota to order the food and organise the transport.

Then there were some last-minute hitches. Gary, who was with the team in Bogota, explains,

The night before it was due to leave for Ecuador, the cargo plane with its Emmanuel TV sticker already in place had to go on an unplanned urgent mission. The sticker dropped off in mid-air! There was a two-day delay while we sourced another sticker and worked with the airline to fix it more securely.

But this setback turned out to be a gift from God. It provided just enough time for the team waiting in Quito, Ecuador's capital, to organise the receiving formalities at the airport and to make more secure arrangements for the transport of the precious cargo of food. Fiona comments,

On the Quito side, time was of the essence, as after waiting for the necessary permissions to be present on the tarmac, we faced the Quito traffic with little time to spare.

We called Gary, who was already with the pilots in the cockpit of the plane, "Can't you hold on? We are running late to get to the airport." His answer was a firm "No, we are already taxiing down the runway!"

Our driver drove like Jehu (2 Kings 9:20), and we all reached the tarmac just in time to see the Emmanuel TV cargo plane descending. The local cameraman got out his camera with seconds to spare. What a moment!

Arrival in Quito of the Cargo Plane with Emmanuel TV Relief Aid

Next, the complicated administration to keep our goods safely in the customs warehouse, clear them, and thence to load them into two army trucks, courtesy of the Ecuadorian army who supplied the trucks and drivers to transport the aid to the earthquake-affected area securely.

Once our large quantity of supplies was safely in the Emmanuel TV local storage area, we visited the official Government Emergency Planning meeting to explain how we wanted to work closely with the Government but to administer the supplies' distribution ourselves. To God be the glory, a happy scheme was worked out. The aims set by T.B. Joshua, to work with the Government, to bring in the Cargo plane, but of course to oversee the distribution of the aid to make sure it got to the right people, was about to come to pass. At the beginning, it had seemed impossible, but now it was happening before our eyes.

Emmanuel TV Team with the Governor of Esmeraldas Province

Gary comments on what seems to have become a regular feature of such ventures of faith,

A combination of extreme challenges and extreme blessings: There always seems to come a time when there is a real risk that a project cannot proceed, and then by holding fast, God brings the right person along or changes someone's attitude - and it is frequently at the very last minute!

When we visited the organised camps with the food supplies, we arrived precisely when their supplies were running low. In one shelter, the ladies in the communal kitchen were very animated at seeing the large quantity of fresh vegetables and garlic to flavour their plain diet.

A New School in the Rainforest

So what next? Well, we knew the Chachi needed a school. When the plan finally came in from the architect, it was substantially bigger and better than the previous building. The new plan was for a high-quality structure to accommodate a kindergarten, primary and secondary school with a total of 14 classrooms, as well as kitchen and dining rooms, a teachers room, an admin room and small computer and science labs. It was clear that the budget would be at least double the ballpark figures we had initially floated with the Lagos team - which were already more than the food distribution project had cost so far.

The whole community's future depended on this school, and T.B. Joshua, moved by their plight, committed to funding the ambitious new structure. The architect agreed to offer his firm as the main contractor, which was a strong commitment since visiting the Chachi required more than 10 hours of travelling for him. For the build-ing project itself, which took many months, he had to have a manager living onsite in the rainforest most of the time. He donated his own time for free to express his thanks to God for his earlier breakthrough.

Preparing to Return from San Salvador by Canoe

In the village of San Salvador de los Chachis, there was no mobile phone coverage; one had to drive for hours to the landing place and then hope the message had got through to the village (with its one landline) so that the canoes would be waiting. Then for the return trip, one had to leave San Salvador in plenty of time to be back on the main road before dusk.

Gary and the Architect Discuss the New School Plans

So it was a substantial undertak-ing to pay even a one hour visit to San Salvador.

The architect finalised the comprehensive school plan, and we submitted it to the Government Education Depart-ment just in time before the two-month Emergency help window closed. It was only during such an emergency that external help was allowed by the Government for such a project. The plan was approved, but then there were bureaucratic delays at the local level that could have threatened the whole project. However, again, we experienced God's provision. A 'chance encounter' with the then Vice President of the nation (Jorge Glas) helped clear the way, and the school went ahead to the great benefit of the indigenous Chachi community and the 300 pupils of the school.

The Team Meets Ecuador's Vice President

THE BIG SCHOOL OPENING!

Because of the access problems and the weather, the school rebuilding project took many months. But just a year after the previous school had been severely damaged in the earthquake, the new structure was ready for an official opening ceremony. T.B. Joshua rarely travelled, but he determined to come to Ecuador to open the school personally.

A Military Welcome to Ecuador for Mr and Mrs Joshua

The planning was complex due to the inaccessibility of the school. There were two opening ceremonies - one in Quito for various dignitaries and one at the school itself. The issue of how T.B. Joshua should make the journey to the school raised logistical problems. The military offered to provide a helicopter, but that would have been too dangerous because of the frequent mist and fog up in the Andes mountains, not to mention the heavy tropical rain. In the end, he was to travel by road from Esmeraldas, and even that had significant difficulties - leading to him having to walk with the team for a long stretch in the mud, which was very tiring.

On the morning of the school's opening ceremony, we had been part of an advance team who just managed to make the whole journey to the school by 4x4 vehicle. (Following the school project, the Government had widened the track by the river to San Salvador, and on the few days that were dry enough, the jour-

T.B. Joshua Continues to the School on Foot

ney could be completed by vehicle.) However, while the guests were gathering at the school, the wind picked up - a sure sign the rain was coming. And then it came in torrents, and with no phone coverage, we had no idea what was happening to T.B. Joshua and the rest of the team. We were starting to think the whole event may have to be abandoned when one of the Chachi ran to us, declaring, "I have seen your master walking along the track up there!" On arrival, he went more or less straight into the ceremony.

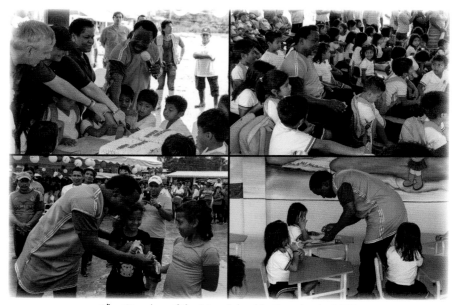

The Opening of the New School in Ecuador in 2017

It was instructive to observe how this indigenous community, relatively untouched by Western norms, demonstrated instinctive respect for the man of God. They seemed to understand that this was an unusual person who was close to God. We were frankly shocked over a year later when, visiting the school for a follow-up project, one of the community leaders respectfully repeated to us some of T.B. Joshua's words of encouragement from that opening ceremony.

On his own side, T.B. Joshua related to the people during that short visit. He proudly wore the traditional Chachi tunic he was presented with, ate the local food, and showed great interest in the farmers' challenges. He sat among the children and personally visited each classroom, writing "Jesus loves you" on the blackboards.

His journey back from the rainforest was also a difficult one, requiring more walking in the mud. He even paid an impromptu visit to one of the local farmers' wooden houses.

He has continued to support the school, fully equipping the computer lab and sponsoring its top student to university, for example.

A CHEERFUL GIVER

There were to be expressions of Emmanuel TV charity all over the world. The UK had no shortage of people with needs of various

Supporting the Flower of Justice in Southampton

kinds, and working with Bob from the Flower of Justice charity in Southampton was a pleasure and honour for us as part of the UK Emmanuel TV charity team.

Bob, a former drug addict, had his life rescued by Jesus and was committed to serving others. He visited The SCOAN with a group in the early years and received significant healing from severe back pain (sciatica). He tells the story in his own book,

> I had had five bleeds in my urine over the year and the doctors couldn't find out what was wrong with me. I was in a lot of pain in my back and I was on painkillers. When T.B. Joshua came to pray for me, he said, 'This is all connected to your past'. He didn't even touch me, but I fell on the floor and I had heat all over my body. I was on my knees, face down, and I couldn't get up because of the power of the Holy Spirit! Then after a bit, he prayed again and said, 'Father, disconnect him from the past!' Then all the pain left my body instantly.[60]

He spoke of his healing to those on the social housing estate where he acted as a street pastor, mentor, and friend of the poor. T.B. Joshua also sent the Emmanuel TV team to conduct regular charity projects on the estate. The result was that many disadvantaged people saw T.B. Joshua as a 'man of the people' who, though thousands of miles away, could relate to their needs.

Providing Local Foods and Essential Supplies for Flood Victims in Laos

The enduring message of charitable giving from T.B. Joshua is that it should be free-spirited. The charitable work of Emmanuel TV around the world would be without 'strings attached', that is, without requiring any particular response from the recipients or the local charities we might partner with. This was much appreciated. Thus it was possible to work with Governments and those who did not share the same faith as us in a joyful way.

Emmanuel TV Sponsors a Traditional English Cream Tea for the Elderly

There have always been many projects providing local foods, from the 'sticky fish' so appreciated by those helped

60   Light, B. (2018). *This is My Offering.* New Life Publishing. p. 86

in Laos, the large bags of flour in Lahore right through to the traditional cream teas so beloved by the English pensioners. Emmanuel TV works sensitively and provides an example for viewers to find for themselves those in need in their local areas and consider how they can help, even if it means starting very simply.

The message from T.B. Joshua, who was passionate about giving to others, is clear,

> "Everyone has something to give. Someone is always there in need of you, no matter how little you have."

LOVE YOUR NEIGHBOUR

Jesus knows us not by our name but by our love. This chapter finishes with a sermon that captures the heart of this man of the people. Love is not a feeling but a practical responsibility for all Christians.

LOVE YOUR NEIGHBOUR

T.B. Joshua, The SCOAN Sunday Service, 9 June 2019

The greatest in the sight of God is the one who loves his neighbour.

"Whoever does not love his brother who he has seen cannot love God who he has not seen, and God has given us this command: Whoever loves God must also love his fellow man." (1 John 4:21)

God measures our lives by our love for Him and for our neighbour. You cannot love God without loving your neighbour. God knows that if you don't really love your neighbour, you cannot love Him. Your neighbour can be your enemy or those who do not share the same faith with you. Let us love one another irrespective of our religion or race, for love comes from God. Whoever does not love does not know God, for God is love (1 John 4:7-8, 11-12).

How can we measure our love for God? By the practical things in our lives. We measure our love for God by the number of times we lovingly think of Jesus daily, by the degree of hunger we have to read His Word, I mean the amount of time we save to read His Word, the joy with which we take His Word in our hands when we are alone with Him. The more we love Him, the more precious His Word will become to us. If you love Jesus enough, you will make it your habit to say, "I love You, Jesus"; when you walk to another room, say "I love You, Jesus"; when you sit down in your car to drive, say "I love You, Jesus"; when you stop at the traffic lights, say "I love You, Jesus". The first person you think of in the morning and the last person you think of at night should be Jesus.

How many things have you adjusted in your life because of your love for God? God says we should not lie; you have stopped lying because you long to please Him; you have stopped destroying because you long to please Jesus, and so on. How do you use your money? How do you economise to give more to the needy? How do you use your free time because you love Jesus? How do you adjust your priorities because of your love for Jesus?

What is the little you try to bless others with because of your love for Jesus? How often do you say, "God bless you"; how often do you deliberately smile at others for Jesus' sake? How often do you try to keep a smile on your face as you drive down the street, as you walk into a store, for Jesus' sake? The more you love God, the more you love your neighbour.

"If you love Me, keep My commandments and I will pray the Father and He will give you another Helper, that He may abide with you forever." (John 14:15-16)

How do we love God? By doing what God wants. We demonstrate our love for Him not with mere words but with action and in truth; that is the way you can demonstrate your love. It is not only coming to church, dancing or reading your Bible; if you love God, keep His commandments. How do we keep God's commandments? We are commanded to love.

God does not ask if you feel like loving. As a Christian, it is our responsibility to love one another. What makes us human is not our ability to think but our ability to love. This means love is life – if you miss love, you miss life. You should not love for selfish, classic or material reasons; we need to love better. If you want to love better, you should start with someone who hates you. If you want to love better, you should start with someone who has bad feelings towards you, who does not see anything good about you, who criticises you; by doing this, you are copying Jesus' kind of love, as He demonstrated in Luke 23:34, *"Father forgive them".*

Take note of the word *them* because it includes both the offender and the offended. In other words, Jesus was saying, "Both the wrong and the right, Father forgive them; both the bad and the good, Father forgive them". If you love many people, but there are those you do not love because they hate you, have bad feelings towards you or criticise you, then your love is as nothing.

"You have heard that it was said that love your neighbour and hate your enemy, but I say to you love your enemies, bless those who curse you, do good to those who hate you and pray for those who spitefully use you and persecute you, that you may be sons of your Father in heaven, for He makes His sun rise on the evil and on the good and sends rain on the just and on the unjust." (Matthew 5:43-45)

God gives the sunshine and rain to all, His blessings of health and long life to all; He loves everybody with the same infinite love with which He loves you. Ask yourself, "To what extent is my love like this?" Nothing makes us love a person so much as praying for them; how many of your neighbours are on your daily prayer list? Is your love a truly interceding love? Can you stand in the gap? Can you rejoice when they rejoice? That is the question for you to answer.

Love frees us in the present. Remember, it is the present that presents problems. It is only through love that we are able to respond to God and others at present. To respond to God first, you must forgive yourself and your neighbours.

Love looks around to see those who are in need. If you don't have love, your faith will not work because faith works by love (Galatians 5:6). It means love is the most important because it is the force that sets faith working.

As Christians, we are known by our love. This means Jesus knows you not by your name but by your love. Love for God's sake does not wait for a reward; when we love for God's sake, we are sowing to the Spirit because the love we give away is the only love we keep.

THE HIGHWAY TO HEAVEN

"If only for this life we have hope in Christ, we are of all people most to be pitied." (1 Corinthians 15:19, NIV)

These words from the Bible are challenging. Most of us are very conscious of this life - we want good health, a well-paid job, a nice place to live in, a happy family etc., and often these are what we are praying to God for. But what will the things of this life count for on the last day, the day when, as C.S. Lewis put it,

> ...the anaesthetic fog which we call "nature" or "the real world" fades away and the Presence in which you have always stood becomes palpable, immediate, and unavoidable?[61]

Both History itself and the faith-filled mentors of yesteryear tell us that life is fragile and that long life or short, we will all come to that final reckoning. How can we respond to this practically, instead of pushing it ever further to the back of our minds?

T.B. Joshua encouraged us to settle all accounts today,

> "We must live each day of our life as if it were our last day because our last day on earth can be so unexpected. Remember, life is uncertain, death is sure, sin is the cause, and Christ is the

---

61   Lewis, C.S. (1952). *Mere Christianity*. Macmillan. p. 115

cure. That life is uncertain should affect the way we live today."

He has taught us that the decisions we should take are those that will benefit our future, not today.

"It is better to suffer today and enjoy tomorrow. God is more concerned with your eternal glory than your present comfort."

There will be trouble in this world (John 16:31) - this is unavoidable. But we should not lose heart,

"For our light and momentary troubles are achieving for us an eternal glory that far outweighs them all." (2 Corinthians 4:17, NIV)

This world is not our home; we are just passing through. Therefore we must not allow our situation to dictate our direction. Our blessings should not determine where we should live or who our friends should be. For example, T.B. Joshua did not relocate to a more prosperous area after the church grew but has allowed God alone to direct his paths.

This outlook has a profound impact on every area of life. The focus in this life is less on enjoying the present and more on remaining faithful to the end. Because it matters how we finish our race.

"In the place where the tree falls, there it shall lie." (Ecclesiastes 11:3)

As the man of God has often stated,

"The beginner is not the owner of the work, but the finisher [is]."

When the time comes for judgement by God, we want to be found in a position of faith so we can enjoy the benefits of eternal salvation through Christ's atoning sacrifice.

What about our attitude to death? If we are not part of the world, and Heaven is our home, then being called home is not something to fear but something to eagerly anticipate. As T.B. Joshua put it,

"Death to a believer is his release from the imprisonment of this world and his departure to the enjoyment of another world.

Those who are born from above long to be there."

Many enthusiastic believers aspire to these truths, but, in reality, we can find ourselves quite at home in this world.

A sermon titled "Time and Season" given by T.B. Joshua in March 2008 helped us personally make that journey from aspiration towards reality. He was teaching on Peter's disappointment at the seaside after an unsuccessful night of fishing before meeting Jesus (Luke 5). A necessary step on the way to reality is to experience the emptiness of the world:

> When we are tired and sick of our worldly business and frustrated in our worldly affairs, we are welcome to Christ. Remember, as long as the world is in place in our lives, Christ must be displaced... He allows us to exhaust whatever worldly advantages we feel we have so that when we have learnt our lessons, we will value Him.

> Jesus would not have had anything to do with Peter had Peter not been made sensible by the vicissitudes of life. He was so tired and sick of the world that he was ready to embrace the superior order of Christ. In Christ's new order, there is peace, not as the world gives.

We thank God that we had experienced enough of the world, including its 'success', to recognise its emptiness. As a contemporary Christian song has put it,

> *This world has nothing for me, and this world has everything. All that I could want, and nothing that I need.*[62]

JUST AS I AM

> *Just as I am, without one plea*
> *But that Thy blood was shed for me*
> *And that Thou bid'st me come to Thee*
> *O Lamb of God, I come! I come*

62　*This World*. Aaron Tate. ©1994 Cumbee Road Music

This famous old hymn which Fiona remembers being sung the night she responded to an altar call in 1973, was also beloved by Billy Graham for his Gospel events. It was sung at The SCOAN in July 2012 at a Memorial Service for President Atta Mills of Ghana, who passed on to glory whilst occupying his country's top office.

The hymn goes on to say,

> *Just as I am, though tossed about*
> *With many a conflict, many a doubt*
> *Fighting and fears within without*
> *O Lamb of God, I come, I come*

> *Just as I am, and waiting not*
> *to rid my soul of one dark blot*
> *to thee whose blood can cleanse each spot*
> *O Lamb of God, I come, I come*

> *Just as I am, poor, wretched, blind*
> *Sight, riches, healing of the mind*
> *Yea, all I need, in Thee to find*
> *O Lamb of God I come, I come*

> *Just as I am, Thou wilt receive*
> *Wilt welcome, pardon, cleanse, relieve*
> *Because Thy promise I believe*
> *O Lamb of God, I come, I come*

The power and reality behind the words are born out of the writer's life lived in pain and sickness yet patient acceptance of God's goodness.

T.B. Joshua said,

> "See your situation as an opportunity to honour God, just as it is an opportunity for God to glorify His name."

Many people greatly admired Charlotte Elliott's hymn, even within her lifetime. Shortly after her death, her brother, the Rev. Henry Venn Elliott, confided in hymnal editor Edward Henry Bickersteth,

"In the course of a long ministry, I hope I have been permitted to see some fruit of my labours, but I feel that far more has been done by a single hymn of my sister's."[63]

Why the example of this hymn? Because Jesus sees the hidden sacrifices and responses to difficulties, not just the outward actions or words. It is the 'force behind the action' that determines the outcome, not the action itself.

As T.B. Joshua challenged his church members, speaking to them at the Prayer Mountain in 2006,

"What will you be remembered for when you pass on to glory? What did people remember the apostles for? Not their wives, children or properties, but the supreme price they paid to bring the Gospel to us. You must be remembered for the purpose for which you were created."[64]

THE HIGHWAY TO HEAVEN

Returning to the Memorial Service for President Atta-Mills, T.B. Joshua gave another encouraging yet sober message,

To get to Heaven, you must follow the way of the Cross. The highway to Heaven starts on this side of death, and the entrance is very easy to find. The Bible says that whoever calls on the name of the Lord shall be saved.

In Romans 10: 1-13, Paul declared that the road to Heaven is not difficult to find nor to access. Are you on the right road to Heaven? It is right in front of you in the Word of God.

In John 14:6, Jesus said, *"I am the way, the truth and the life. No one comes to the Father except through Me."* He died for our sin - broke the power of death by resurrection. You need not fear where you are going when you know Jesus is going with you. You are not alone.

Death is not a full stop; it is only a comma because of Jesus

---

63 Bickersteth E.H. (1872). *Hymnal Companion to the Book of Common Prayer*, Annotated Edition. Sampson Low & Co. Note 114
64 *Responsible Use of Blessings*. Message by T.B. Joshua at Prayer Mountain, 2 Mar 2006

Christ's death and resurrection - If you put your faith in Him. Any day, even today, may be our final day on earth. We need to be sure that we are ready to depart. Are you?

Whether you are young or old, what matters is the grace to continue living hereafter. A man may die young yet be satisfied with living. But a wicked man is not satisfied even with a long life. Continuing to trust God is the only way to get ready for the things we are not ready for.

If you are prepared to die, you are prepared to live. I pray for you that when it is time for you to depart, you will know, in Jesus' name.[65]

What is a Christian?

"A real Christian is anyone who depends on God's grace and puts his trust in Christ alone for salvation."

This is the essence of Christianity, not a religion but a relationship with Jesus Christ by faith. It is a relationship that extends beyond the grave, freeing those *"who all their lives were held in slavery by their fear of death."* (Hebrews 2:15).

Prophet T.B. Joshua regularly reminded his listeners of the fundamentals of the faith. For his 2020 Easter message, preached from the Emmanuel TV Studios, he addressed the question head on: *What is a Christian?*

As a minister of God, I have seen that people give numerous reasons for calling themselves Christians. For instance, they say, "I was born a Christian, and I grew up in the church." "I am a Christian because my parents are believers." "I am a Christian because I am a publisher of the Bible." "I am a Christian because I am convinced that Jesus is the Son of God." My problem with these answers is that they don't mention the only reason that qualifies someone as a Christian.

Here is the challenge. You can attend church and not be a Christian. You can read the Bible and not be a Christian. You

---

can eliminate bad habits and try to be a moral person and still not be a Christian. All these habits are good, but the actions alone do not make a person a Christian.

Who is a Christian then? A Christian is a person whom God has forgiven through the finished work of Jesus Christ on the Cross, as the Book of Titus 3:3-6 said. We are Christians because of the finished work of Jesus Christ on the Cross. Man is a sinner who has fallen short of God's standard. God came to the earth in the person of Jesus Christ, died for us and paid for our sin. Through our faith in Him, we receive His right-eousness, and we receive His forgiveness of our sins and the gift of eternal life.

Jesus died on the Cross for me and you. He died for us, He loves us, and when we open our heart, He forgives us. Let me take you to the Book of Acts of the Apostles, chapter 16 verses 30 to 31. This is the case of a law enforcement officer who once asked Apostle Paul the most important question: What must I do to be saved? Paul answered, "Believe in the Lord Jesus; you will be saved." Here is the point: Being a Christian is not about what you do; it is about what Christ Jesus has done. He loves us, He died for us, and He forgives us when we open our hearts to believe.[66]

PRAYERS OF DEDICATION

If you have not known the Lord Jesus, or if you want to rededicate your life to Him, you can pray this prayer:

Lord Jesus, I need you.
I am a sinner.
Come into my heart;
Wash me with Your precious blood.
Save my soul today,
In the name of Jesus Christ.

If you have submitted to God's will and want to know more of His

---

66   *What is a Christian?* Message by T.B. Joshua, Emmanuel TV Sunday Live Broadcast, 12 Apr 2020

direction for your life, you can pray:

> *Lord Jesus, I have given up to Your will;*
> *I am ready to go wherever You want me to go,*
> *To say whatever You want me to say,*
> *To be whatever You want me to be.*
> *I am ready, Lord; I am ready now!*
> *The time is short – the world is coming to an end.*
> *I don't want to waste my time.*
> *Tell me what I should do.*
> *Give me Your orders.*
> *I promise to submit myself to all that You desire of me*
> *And to accept all that You permit to happen to me.*
> *Let me only know Your will.*

T.B. Joshua always encouraged new believers to look for a living church and to get involved there. But remember, the essence of the true church is Christ in you, the hope of glory. On Judgement Day, the question will not be who worshipped at this church or that church, or who is a bishop or pastor or prophet, but who worshipped God in spirit and truth (John 4:24). What matters is the state of your heart.

You need to ask yourself this question: Are you living each day as if it were your last?

How are you using your life? How are you spending your life? Because the greatest way to use life is to spend it on something that will outlive it. For instance, love someone more dearly every day. When you look around you, you will see someone who needs something you possess - your love, your help, strength, your time, your smile, or your word of encouragement to guide them on the right path.

To keep our heart fit for His holy sight and to answer when He calls - this is our task.

Live each day as if it were your last. Some day, you will be right.

EPILOGUE

T.B. Joshua was a prophet of our time who taught the Word of God, bringing conviction - conviction of sin and the need to become more serious about following God; an assurance that God is real and that Jesus Christ is coming back soon.

The Word of God dominated his thinking, as reflected in the way he handled hard times and opposition to the Gospel. Calmly he would say, "I see things differently", and his words promoted peace.

There have always been such 'Fathers in the Lord', who are nonconforming (and hence controversial) in their own time, but whose spiritual legacies have the potential to shape future generations.

There is a pressing need today in Christendom for the uniting of the effective application of the Word of God and the demonstration of the Holy Spirit in power. We have seen consistent evidence of this over the past two decades.

Even so, T.B. Joshua made it very clear that he had not yet 'arrived'; he was still pressing on for more of God, and who knows what the future holds?

"Most assuredly, I say to you, he who believes in Me, the works that I do he will do also; and greater works than these he will do, because I go to My Father." (John 14:12)

Throughout the years, he had made no secret of his desire to see people in ministry go further than he had done. He poured his life effort into mentoring people;

> "How strange, yet wholly true; the weak filled with the power of God, the Father's work shall do!"

For those whose lives are centred in Christ Jesus, the best is always yet to come!

About the Authors

 Gary and Fiona Tonge were born in England in the late 1950s. By 1973, when the 'Jesus Movement' brought a wave of renewal, they both experienced an encounter with Jesus Christ that radically changed the direction of their lives. Taking an active role in church life as elders, lay preachers and youth leaders, they had the privilege of travelling to see the power of God in evidence in healing and deliverance in different parts of the world in the 1990s and early 2000s.

Gary gained a first-class honours degree in Electronics and a PhD in Mathematics from the University of Southampton. He enjoyed a successful career, joining the Management Board of the UK Independent Television Commission (ITC) in his early 30s, before launching out into consultancy and voluntary Christian work from 2004. A Chartered Engineer of over 35 years, he is a Fellow of the Royal Academy of Engineering and of the Institution of Engineering and Technology.

Fiona is a former nurse with a recent Postgraduate Diploma in International Disaster Management from the University of Manchester.

For the past two decades, they travelled for T.B. Joshua as part of Emmanuel TV teams to prepare for stadium gospel events and to coordinate humanitarian projects around the world.